Praise for *CHASING WONDER*

"Ginger is an engaging storyteller who has done an excellent job sharing the amazing adventures she has had in her life to illustrate her passion for an awareness of the wonder we too often miss. I believe reading her book will give you a new hunger for more adventure in your own life and lead you in practical steps you can take to get there. The book is well written; it will make you laugh in some places and perhaps cry in others. It will also help to bring you closer to God."

—Joyce Meyer

"The thing I love most about Ginger is that her genuine and kind spirit is always radiating joy. In this book she'll take you on a journey through her own experiences and teach you how to cultivate a mind-set of adventure and joy in your own life. A fulfilling life of adventure starts with having an identity rooted in Christ, so Ginger not only shares biblical wisdom but also provides practical checklists and tools for you to move towards living a life full of awe and wonder."

—Natalie Grant, recording artist

"As Jesus followers, we've been invited to live an abundant life. *Chasing Wonder* dares us to step into the fullness of our purpose right where we are. You'll be inspired and activated to embrace the wonder of a faith-filled life in Christ."

—Christine Caine, founder of A21 and Propel Women

"This is such an energizing read. With a heart full of wonder, Ginger encourages us to approach life and faith as a grand adventure—embracing all of its beauty and messiness. *Chasing Wonder* is a joy to journey through and will revitalize so many hearts. If you're needing a push—or simply permission—to step into a life of heightened faith and adventure, this is the book for you."

—Matt and Beth Redman, songwriters-authors

"I have always admired Ginger, her ministry, and her way with words. Her book, *Chasing Wonder*, is just what you need to inspire you, encourage you, and help bring adventure and joy into your everyday life! I highly recommend Ginger's book and know that God has a message for you through *Chasing Wonder*."

—Lisa Osteen Comes, associate pastor, Lakewood Church, and author of *You Are Made for More!*

"Between the overwhelming daily barrage of information from social media, mobile phones, and more, we live in the most distracted and cluttered culture in history—which means there's never been a more important moment for us to recapture a sense of "wonder" than right now. And that's exactly why Ginger Stache's new book, *Chasing Wonder: Small Steps toward a Life of Big Adventures*, is so important. In this amazing book, you'll discover how to get back in touch with that magical feeling you felt as a child—the attitude that nothing is impossible and everything is yours for the taking. If your life is growing stale, boring, or if you've lost your ability to dream, then this book is for you. Buy it. Read it. The world needs more people who believe."

—Phil Cooke, PhD, media producer, filmmaker, and author of *One Big Thing: Discovering What You Were Born to Do*

"How many of us might have let our lives settle into the mundane and the routine and then realize we are just a bit bored? Or perhaps if we were honest, we recognize that wrestle with regret. In *Chasing Wonder*, Ginger Stache challenges us to seek the adventure and to rekindle the wonder. Using her very warm style, she tells stories and offers practical help in reclaiming the life we were created to live."

—Holly Wagner, pastor, author, teacher, founder of She Rises

"Ginger will inspire all who read this amazing story of her own personal journey not to settle for less than what God has planned for you. I believe you will be deeply moved and stirred to take those small steps of faith that will take you on your own personal adventure in life. As I read Ginger's words, I felt a deeper passion to take time to love people well so their lives are changed forever."

—Nancy Alcorn, founder and president, Mercy Multiplied

"We all want to live a life full of joy. Ginger brings joy to whatever she faces in life, and she helps us find the secrets to finding delight in not only the big moments of life but in the everyday and even difficult moments. Her story is amusing and moving, and reading it was a pleasure."

—Shelly Meyer, international relations officer, Hand of Hope

"Successful media projects are about choosing a story that takes an audience on an unforgettable adventure. It's called the 'WOW' factor. In her remarkable new book, Ginger Stache opens our eyes to understanding how to know and trust God more deeply. God's story is the biggest 'WOW' factor ever, and *Chasing Wonder* will help guide you into taking the greatest adventure of your life."

—Kathleen Cooke, cofounder, Cooke Media Group and The Influence Lab, author of *Hope 4 Today: Stay Connected to God in a Distracted Culture*

"This book does a great job of motivating us all to not settle for anything less than God's best. Ginger has been a huge blessing to the ministry and our family. She has helped tell the story in amazing ways over the years. I highly encourage you to read *Chasing Wonder*."

—David L. Meyer, CEO, Hand of Hope

"In *Chasing Wonder*, Ginger shows how to 'stop being prisoners of circumstance.' If you want to live a life of wonder, she explains how simple it really is. This is a must-read book for everyone, especially if you are (deep down) tired and/or bored."

—Pat Bradley, cofounder, Crisis Aid International

"A master storyteller, my friend Ginger takes you on a delightful journey full of laughter and tears. And the best part is, along the way you'll discover the keys and the inspiration to propel you on your own amazing journey of wonder and joy. Give your life the spark you're looking for! I loved *Chasing Wonder* and am happy to recommend it!"

—Lisa Bevere, *New York Times* bestselling author

CHASING WONDER

CHASING WONDER

SMALL STEPS
TOWARD A LIFE OF
BIG ADVENTURES

GINGER STACHE

WORTHY

PUBLISHING

New York • Nashville

Worthy
Hachette Book Group
1290 Avenue of the Americas, New York, NY 10104
worthypublishing.com
twitter.com/worthypub

First edition: June 2021

Worthy is a division of Hachette Book Group, Inc. The Worthy name and logo are trademarks
of Hachette Book Group, Inc.

The publisher is not responsible for websites (or their content) that are not owned by the
publisher.

The Hachette Speakers Bureau provides a wide range of authors for speaking events. To find
out more, go to www.hachettespeakersbureau.com or call (866) 376-6591.

Unless otherwise indicated, scriptures are taken from The ESV® Bible (the Holy Bible, English
Standard Version®). ESV® Text Edition: 2016. Copyright © 2001 by Crossway, a publishing
ministry of Good News Publishers.

Library of Congress Cataloging-in-Publication Data

Names: Stache, Ginger, author.
Title: Chasing wonder : small steps toward a life of big adventures / Ginger Stache.
Description: First edition. | New York : Worthy, 2021. | Includes bibliographical references.
Identifiers: LCCN 2020054036 | ISBN 9781546029472 (hardcover) | ISBN 9781546029489
    (ebook)
Subjects: LCSH: Christian life. | Wonder. | Conduct of life.
Classification: LCC BV4501.3 .S7225 2021 | DDC 248.4—dc23
LC record available at https://lccn.loc.gov/2020054036

ISBNs: 978-1-5460-2947-2 (hardcover), 978-1-5460-2948-9 (ebook)

Printed in the United States of America

LSC-W

Printing 1, 2021

*To my parents, Jack and Linda Cunnington,
who passed their adventure mentalities along
to me. Thank you for being my greatest
cheerleaders, for showing me that there is
a great big world of wonder out there to
discover, and for being constant
examples of God's love.*

And amazement seized them all, and they glorified
God and were filled with awe, saying,
"We have seen extraordinary things today."
—Luke 5:26—

The purpose of life, after all, is to live it, to taste
experience to the utmost, to reach out eagerly
and without fear for newer and richer experience.
—Eleanor Roosevelt—

CONTENTS

FOREWORD

Ginger is both a good friend and a valuable coworker. I've known her for almost twenty years, and I can say without hesitation that she is one of the most creative people I know. She loves the Lord with all her heart, and she loves people. She also loves adventure!

In this book she will inspire a hunger in you for new adventures of your own and a desire to see the wonder all around you. The book is well written; it will make you laugh in some places and perhaps cry in others. It will also help to bring you closer to God.

Ginger is an engaging storyteller who has done an excellent job sharing the amazing adventures she has had in her life to illustrate her passion for an awareness of the wonder we too often miss. I believe reading her book will give you a new hunger for more adventure in your own life and lead you in practical steps you can take to get there. It will help you to be very thankful for what you have, be more generous, and deal with pride and impure motives. And these are only a few of the spiritual lessons you will learn while she takes you on amazing journeys everywhere—from the top of a mountain to a grass hut in a jungle complete with an army of creepy-crawly things that kept her company at night.

Ginger is a sincere, authentic woman of God who wants to make—and is making—a positive difference in many people's lives. I highly recommend *Chasing Wonder* and I'm honored to write the foreword to this creative, fresh approach to making all of life an adventure.

Joyce Meyer

INTRODUCTION

It was one of the first adventures I can remember, and it could have been my last—a harrowing experience. I'll tell you all about it in chapter one, but for now let's just say that I went out on a limb…way too far out. As I think back on my eight-year-old self and this experience of hanging on for dear life, I vividly remember two things: looking down and seeing no ground beneath me and a rush of excitement.

Life is meant to be a grand adventure. It should surprise and wow us on a regular basis and be full of awe and wonder. There is plenty of wonder to be found; the problem is our days are so full of routine, monotony, and fear, that it is easier to stay on that treadmill of boredom than it is to step off into the unknown and discover something wonderful. In the Bible, Jesus promises in John 10:10 that He came so that we could love the life that God gives us. He says that He came so that we could have a big life, abundant with wondrous moments. Yet He gives us choices. We can take the easy way, moving from day to day, following a prescribed schedule of tedium, or we can perhaps go out on a limb—push just a little, get out there, and see what wonder God has in store for us!

Is anything I am saying connecting with you? Do you feel as if you are missing some of the best parts of life, including adventures of your own because you are stuck in a cycle of robotically moving from one responsibility to the next? Is fear keeping you from experiences that could bring you the joy you've always desired? Is it possible you've grown complacent with "good enough" when God wants to show you "extraordinary"?

If so, come along with me and together we'll explore the adventures and misadventures of this wide-eyed traveler. Believe me, I've learned a lot, and yes, some of my lessons came much harder than others. Perhaps the greatest—the truth that ties all the others together through it all—is that God has undeniable wonder in store for us. Incredible things like outrageous beauty, astounding surprises, heartwarming kindness, laughing-till-you-pee-a-little enjoyment, and awestruck silence as you simply take it all in.

I have also discovered that this wonder can be elusive—after all, if it was easy to come by it wouldn't be all that exceptional, would it? If we aren't really looking, if we are distracted by the noise and clutter, or consumed by the very real pain of life, wonder fades quietly into the background and passes without notice. These extraordinary moments God has for you may be on the other side of the world or hidden in plain sight. If we don't make the effort to get up and go after it, the wonder of this life goes on without us. In fact, encountering it requires some chasing. We must pursue wonder like we would a great opportunity or a lost treasure.

Throughout my life as a wife and mother, my professional experiences, escapades with other cultures and landscapes, and a great deal of trial and error, I've gathered some extremely valuable lessons. And I'm willing to share them all—the highs and the lows. I welcome this vulnerability, and yes, potential embarrassment because I have personally benefited from the experiences shared by so many others who came before me. I've learned from them and been incredibly inspired. We need each other and we have so much to learn together through sharing our stories.

I promise you this: I will be open, honest, and down-to-earth. I'm not a theologian or a counselor—I'm a creative at heart, a television producer, a writer, a traveler, and a lover of people. I approach this as a friend, walking through life together, sitting down for a cup of hot chocolate (I don't like coffee, but I'm happy to pick up one for you), and sharing her experiences with you. The kind of friend who loves you enough to give you a good kick in the pants when you need some loving motivation.

So, what do you say? Shall we agree to embark on this

adventure together and go chasing wonder? The path might get a bit bumpy, but I promise you, it will be worth it. I believe along the way you will uncover the steps you can take to discover your own incredible adventures, and open your eyes to a deeper awareness of the beautiful and amazing things God has in store for you. There is a big, wonderful life ahead!

SECTION I

AN ADVENTURE MENTALITY

Life is either a great adventure or nothing at all.
—Helen Keller—

CHAPTER 1

OUT ON A LIMB

You've got to go out on a limb sometimes
because that's where the fruit is.
—Will Rogers—

When I looked out the small plane's window, all I could see was rugged mountainside. Where on earth were we going to land? We were in Papua New Guinea, flying over stunningly beautiful terrain on our way to visit a remote village in the highlands. Suddenly it appeared, a tiny grass runway carved into the side of the mountain. No. Way. We touched down, hit the brakes hard, and bumped to a stop. It was intense, and I thought that would be the most extraordinary moment of the day. I was wrong.

Soon, the door was open, and we were greeted by a tribe of amazing people with broad smiles. I was instantly captivated by these men, women, and children who were wearing beautiful beads, grasses, flowers, and colorful paint. Not costumes, but their Sunday best. They invited us into their community meeting lodge, and as we were walking toward it we were startled by sounds of yelling, whooping, and hollering. When I looked up, I saw a group of tribesmen running toward us at full speed, spears above their heads pointed directly at us, and war cries bellowing. It was a shocking and unforgettable sight.

They continued running toward us and as they got closer, we could see the intense expressions on their painted faces. We were invited guests in this village, so while I wasn't afraid, my heart definitely skipped a beat or two. Some people in our group reacted more strongly. There may have been some slightly damp undergarments.

As the men ran past us and everyone in the village cheered, the full revelation sunk in that absolutely no harm was intended; actually, quite the opposite was true. Our friends from this tiny village named Tsediap had planned a welcome like none we have ever experienced. They understood something that more people should—they knew that deep down, people want memorable, remarkable experiences. They believed in adventure—and they were providing us with one we would never forget. They were giving us a gift.

Best gift ever! It still makes me smile.

I believe in adventure too. Big ones, small ones, and everything in between. And this was one of my favorites. Our adventures become the memories we cherish and the stories we share. They inspire us, teach us, motivate us, and open the door to wonder. We need adventure in our life. You don't necessarily need a tribe of men threatening you with spears, but you do need moments of the extraordinary.

I've been passionate about living adventurously as long as I can remember. I recall one of my earliest adventures, and unlike the one in Tsediap, I was very much afraid. In fact, I was paralyzed with fear—I had gone too far out on a limb, quite literally. I remember holding on to a tree branch with a death grip and looking down to see my little Chuck Taylor All-Star tennis shoes dangling beneath me and no ground below. There was nothing but the sharply dropping mountainside. I turned and could see no way back. This adventure had gone very wrong.

I was around eight years old and hiking with my parents in the Great Smoky Mountains National Park. I ran ahead on the trail and saw a tree growing crookedly out of the side of the mountain. I wasn't very tall, I was eight after all, so I started climbing for a better view. It seemed like a really good idea, but when I found myself clinging to that limb for dear life, not so much.

I heard my dad calling me back toward him, gently at first. "Ginger, scoot back this way. You can do it." Then both my mom and dad's voices became much more…let's say *insistent*. "Young lady, get down here now." They had told me to stay with them and away from the edge, but that tree was simply too enticing. Before I knew it, I had climbed out to the farthest point and was looking down, way down, over the steep ledge. And that's when it happened: the paralyzing fear set in, along with the realization that getting back from a place isn't always as easy as getting there.

I remember hearing them calling to me, "You're going to have to do this yourself." You see, the limb was too small to hold anyone else's weight, so they couldn't climb out to get me. I had gotten myself into this mess, and I had to make my own way back. As the limb swayed in the light breeze, I could hear cracking noises beneath me. I had two options: I could at least attempt to get back the way I had come or take the very quick way down. Option two did not appeal to me at all.

I'm honestly not sure how, but I remember forcing my little body to move, inch by inch, and in a snaillike fashion, shimmying back until my dad's arms wrapped around me and pulled me from the branch. I was safe, and when my heart finally stopped racing and the fear subsided, I remember thinking, "That was awesome!"

Now, this probably wasn't the first and was absolutely *not* the last time I ran ahead. I still tend to venture out onto limbs. It's a personality trait, I suppose, and one that has led to many wonderful life lessons and a few difficult ones over the years. Climbing out onto this limb is, perhaps, a metaphor for my life, representing the good traits as well as the "opportunities for growth," as I like to call them. I love the view from the edge and a grand experience, and perhaps most of all, I have come to appreciate a passion for adventure.

This girl from small-town Indiana has traveled the world, met fascinating people, enjoyed a family I adore and a career I love. I have witnessed things few people get to be part of and visited places most never see. I have experienced great joy and desperate heartache. I've lived a lot. I've soaked in a lot of wonder. And many more adventures lie ahead.

I firmly believe we are at our best when we live with an attitude that life should be an adventure—an outlook that sets the stage by believing every moment has the potential to bring something amazing, a sight to behold, or a lesson to be learned. When we make room in our lives for adventure, we open the door to greater wonder, bigger joy, and space for God to move in ways we may have never experienced otherwise.

I call this outlook on life an "adventure mentality." It's a mindset of expectancy, anticipating wonderful possibilities ahead, along with a willingness to stretch in order to experience something new and extraordinary. And anybody can develop it. This adventure mentality is a firm understanding that the best things in life often come with a little extra effort, and a readiness to at least check it out to see. Life is full of wonder, amazing moments, and experiences God created for us to soak up. So glorious, it's not enough to just visit this wonder—it's far better to chase after it and to live there!

Merriam-Webster defines *wonder* as "a cause of astonishment," "a marvel," "a miracle." "Rapt attention at something awesomely mysterious or new to one's experience."[1] That definition intrigues me—those are things I don't want to miss, and I believe they are things God has in store for all of us. In fact, that definition pretty well sums up a life of big adventure. So for me, the chase is on!

I always like to say, "Have a strategy." So as we begin chasing wonder together, step one is to begin nurturing this adventure mentality. You've probably heard the phrase "a spirit of adventure" and it is an important aspect of this, but a mentality goes beyond that. A spirit of adventure can come and go with feelings or moods, but a *mentality* reflects your core, your foundation. It's a decision that goes much deeper than your feelings; you set your mind and keep it set. It determines how you see life and how you interact with others.

Why do you need adventure, you ask? You can certainly survive without it—keep your head down and live in your comfort zone, doing only what you must to maintain the day-to-day. But perhaps the better question is, what do you want from your life? Is maintaining good enough? I believe you can reach beyond what is expected of you, and what you may be expecting of yourself. You can live a big life. And I firmly believe God wants that for you as well. He wants to open your world to big wonder.

In Jeremiah 33:3, God told Jeremiah, "Call to me and I will answer you, and will tell you great and hidden things that you have not known." Now that sounds like a great adventure to me! Hidden treasure! God wants to amaze and surprise you. You should be energized and motivated. You don't have to settle for bored, disappointed, and discouraged.

You weren't born to be like everyone else. I remember reading a quote from Oprah Winfrey saying she always knew she was destined for greatness. My friend, author and Bible teacher Joyce Meyer, said she knew, even as a child growing up in a home filled with anger and abuse, that one day she would do something great. I am certainly nothing special, but I remember always believing that God had something wonderful and very specific planned just for me. But here is what you may not know—He has all these things for you too. You weren't born just to fade into the background. God loves you just as much. And He has amazing adventures planned for YOU.

You want to be happy, and believe it or not, God wants that for you too. He wants to share His wonder with you. John 10:10 says that He came so you can have life and enjoy it. God is uncontainable. Stop trying to fit Him into your tiny box. Instead, you can be a part of His big world. Open your doors to living big adventures with Him. It isn't frivolous or extravagant. He says you are worth it, so reach for the extraordinary. Otherwise the life He wants you to enjoy may be choked out by the weeds of monotony, slowly withering as you become smaller and smaller. He wants you to be inspired and to be an inspiration. He offers everything you need to build a life you love. To fight isolation, sadness, and loneliness. To stretch to reach your potential.

You may be skeptical, thinking I don't really know you…but as I'm writing, I feel like I do. Deep down we all want the same things. When I'm on television and looking into that camera lens, I am talking to real people, friends I can see in my mind's eye.

Lovely friends who may be hurting, afraid, bored with life, or simply seeking more.

Your dreams may have been squelched and your trust and confidence crushed, but you are not alone or unseen. There is more for you. And I know this about you because God says in His Word that it is true for each and every one of us.

So…are you ready to begin a new phase of life? No matter how young or old you are God can lead you to new and amazing experiences that fit you perfectly. Put aside your previous ideas of adventure, and let's look at it together from a completely new perspective. It begins with a decision to live hungry for all the wonder God has for you.

CHOOSE YOUR OWN ADVENTURE

I told you I love the view from the edge. One of my very favorite things is to hike or climb or fly to a high vantage point where the vista is expansive, and you can't help but stand in awe. I am one of those people who relish standing close to the edge and taking in all that beauty. I sit and let my feet swing freely over the ledge, or I lie flat on my belly and look down, hanging my head over for the full experience. My husband, Tim, on the other hand, stands back and enjoys the panorama from a comfortable distance. I love the exhilarating freedom and a little surge of adrenaline, while he enjoys the view from his own safe perspective. He follows the rules and I may push the limits just a bit, but we both have an adventure mentality. We are both standing on that mountaintop.

You see, I'm talking about a mindset rather than a location or a physical position. A great adventure for me may be to swim with sharks while yours might be to simply get in the water in the first place. My idea of adventure may be different from yours, or yours may be far more extreme than mine, but what people with an adventure mentality have in common is a desire to experience life deeply. To soak in all the love and joy they possibly can and to have enough overflowing to share with others.

You can embody this passion, do it in your own way, and be led by God's Holy Spirit. You can live with an adventure mentality and you don't have to do it just like me or anyone else, but you do have to make a conscious effort. I'm not asking you to follow anyone else's path. I'm asking you to blaze your own with a willingness to stretch just a bit more than you normally would. To go out on that limb a little bit further than you may have before.

Let's explore some valuable lessons I learned back in that tree on the mountainside:

- Don't venture out on a weak limb.
- You can be afraid yet overcome paralyzing fear.
- My father would always be there to catch me.
- Life is best when lived just a bit on the edge.

A sound you do *not* want to hear is that branch creaking beneath you, so whatever you do, make sure you carefully check it out before climbing out too far. Are you choosing the right branch? Is it sturdy enough to hold the weight of your decision?

I am not encouraging you to be careless, but to cast your cares on God, who is with you and has a brilliant path just for you. We know His plans for one are not the same as they are for another, but His plan for each of us is always good (see Jer. 29:11). So, don't attempt to follow exactly in the footsteps of another; that branch may be right for them, but not for you, and vice versa. This life of adventure is not a competition; it revolves around a relationship between God and you.

I may be a leaper and you may be a lagger, or you may have already jumped while I'm still holding on for dear life, and that's okay, as long as we have this one important thing in common— trust in our loving heavenly Father who will always be there to catch us. Just like my dad pulled me safely from that tree limb on the mountainside, my heavenly Father has always been there with His arms stretched out to help me, and He is always there for you too. Even if your earthly father hasn't been.

Romans 8:38–39 says: "For I am sure that neither death nor life, nor angels nor rulers, nor things present nor things to come, nor powers, nor height nor depth, nor anything else in all creation, will be able to separate us from the love of God in Christ Jesus our Lord." Every time I read that I am awestruck. It is God's promise to us that our heavenly Father will always be there to catch us.

Trusting Him defeats the fear that inevitably attempts to stop us in our tracks. And fear may be the number one enemy of adventure, telling us it is too foolish or risky or that we might fail. If fear is keeping you from your adventures, just consider the danger of a life of monotony—relentless routine makes for a slow, painful death. But you can move in the face of fear, and you must. Joyce Meyer calls it, "doing it afraid." It's not the presence or feeling of fear that defeats you, it is allowing the fear to stop you from doing what you should. Which brings us back to trust in the faithfulness of God. We can "do it afraid" because our trust is in a trustworthy God.

FAITHFUL SNEAKERS

There is something very comforting to me about my Converse Chuck Taylor All-Stars. I wore them climbing that tree and on countless other adventures through the years (though not the same exact pair, of course). While those flat soles were not great for climbing trees, they were made for the basketball court. I grew up in Indiana where playing basketball was a part of life, and they were the go-to sneaker. Somewhere along the way they became popular on and off the court, and I was at home in them everywhere, from those early days exploring the neighborhood on my bicycle, through the ups and downs of high school. I was learning to trust God with every step.

Today, more years later than I care to say, I still love my classic Chucks. They are comfortable, dependable, and work with most any outfit. Who doesn't love a fun summer dress with a pair of cute kicks? My faithful Chucks are just kind of "me."

I am very thankful for those memories in my Chucks. They remind me of God's faithfulness walking with me through the years, how He has guided, comforted, and pursued me. I remember how He was with me through every adventure and every heartache, and how He patiently waited for me. With each step I grew comfortably more familiar with His character—an adventure that continues to this day.

Every day, I am still reminded of God's unwavering faithfulness. A bit like my Chucks, He is dependable, comfortable, and never goes out of style. God's love for me through the years is the foundation of who I am. Just kind of "me."

This adventure mentality—this desire for new experiences, continuing growth, and a willingness to challenge myself—is only possible because I trust my life is secure in God's hands. There are no guarantees for any of us along this journey, with this one exception: God's Word is faithful. Always. My adventures, my purpose, and my future are safe with Him, and His desire for me is to live a life that widens my eyes in wonder on a regular basis.

What are your dreams for your life? It is important to have

aspirations such as achieving an educational degree or landing that career you've always wanted, and an adventure mentality will *certainly* help you to achieve those goals, but I'm asking you something deeper. What would your life look like in your very best dreams? Have you ever even considered that? Would you spend more time with people you love? Would you have more joy and peace? Would you laugh a lot and take pleasure in seeing and experiencing amazing things? Would your life be fulfilled and meaningful?

God wants these things for you. Psalm 37:4 says, "Delight yourself in the LORD, and he will give you the desires of your heart." It sounds pretty good to think this means God will give us everything we want, but I don't believe that is what this scripture is saying. What it does promise is even better: If you delight in God, or focus on and enjoy Him, then He will place in your heart a desire for the things that matter most. He will cause you to want the things that line up with His Word and His plan for you. How fabulous! If we love God so much that we take great pleasure in Him, He will fill our heart with the desires that will bring us the greatest joy. Our job is to chase after those desires.

Allow me to push you just a little as you journey through the pages of this book. It's what good friends do, and always with great love. I promise these friendly little nudges toward adventure and your own pursuit of wonder won't hurt much, but they just may be the encouragement you need.

Merriam-Webster defines *adventure* as "an undertaking usually involving danger and unknown risks," "the encountering of risks," "an exciting or remarkable experience." I read this as "wonder."

It's time for a little nudge out of your norm. So much wonder is out there calling for you to soak it in, but it's not waiting for you. You've got to chase after it! You don't have to do anything too crazy, but I am asking you to risk a little more of the unknown in order to step into your remarkable experiences. I want you to be in awe of God's goodness, His majesty and creativity, His unprecedented love for you each and every day. And when you are, He will bless you with a heart that desires more of Him, more of His astounding adventures, more joy and love spilling out into other people's lives. *That is an adventure mentality.* That is what you can have, and life is definitely better when lived just a bit on the edge, because that is where we see so much more of God.

STEP BY STEP

- Write out a description of your life in your happiest dreams.
- Choose your own adventure—something that is right for you at this time.
- Baby steps can be great adventures. Here are some suggestions to start small:
    - Buy a different cereal.
    - Rearrange the furniture.
    - Talk to a neighbor you don't know well.
    - Ask God to show you something new.
- Don't push yourself too far, too fast. Develop your trust muscle and allow God to show He is faithful to you.
- As you're warming up, try something a bit bigger:
    - Plan an outing.
    - Apply for that job you want.
    - Say what you've needed to say.
    - Ask God to show you something amazing.
- Delight in the Lord and step out on your first adventure. You're developing your adventure mentality!

CHAPTER 2

IMPOSSIBLY WONDERFUL

It always seems impossible until it's done.

—Nelson Mandela—

Our family was traveling in the desert outside of Casablanca, Morocco, toward the Atlas Mountains when we saw an absolutely crazy sight. It was one of those things that stopped us dead in our tracks and made us do a double take because we couldn't believe our eyes. I felt like I was seeing a Photoshopped image, but then I remembered this was real life. (I wish Photoshop worked in real life. How awesome would that be? But it does not.) This was a *Ripley's Believe It or Not!* kind of moment.

There was a field containing several bushy, thorny trees, about twenty feet tall. These trees were full of goats. Not birds, not squirrels—*goats*. And I'm not talking about your typical goats hanging out on the ground at the base of the trees; these goats were actually climbing the trees. They were all over them, standing on the tiny branches throughout, all the way to the top. Some trees had as many as ten goats climbing in them.

So many questions! How did these hoofed, ground-dwelling creatures do it? And which was the first goat standing on the ground below to look up at the branches and say, "I'm going up there"? Did he or she take flak from the others? "Wait a minute, Pat, are you crazy? Look at your spindly legs and tiny hooves. It's not like you have opposable thumbs or a long tail for holding on to a branch. This is not going to work!" And then, they probably threw out that classic statement, "We've always been down here, and we should stay down here."

Evidently undaunted by the jeers of the crowd and looking for something new and better, I imagine Pat began the climb. Step by step, Pat began to realize what was always considered impossible was in fact not, and the payoff for this adventurous determination was a delicious meal of once unreachable fruit. When the other goats looked up in absolute amazement and saw Pat standing at the top of that tree, they must have followed suit, changing their lives for generations to come. And what do I imagine those goats from Casablanca probably said? "Well done, Pat. Here's looking at you, kid."

How many adventures do we miss out on because we've been

told it isn't possible? How many wonderful opportunities and amazing things do we say no to because no one else we know is doing it? Jesus said in Matthew 19:26, "With man this is impossible, but with God all things are possible." We are not bound by the limits others place upon us or even the boundaries we often put on ourselves. If we can shed those preconceived ideas of what we *can* or *should* do and instead offer God a heart open to anything and everything He wants for us, like those Moroccan goats, it can change us and generations to come.

I had yet one more question concerning these innovative goats: What was so enticing at the top of that tree that it drew them to do the impossible? I learned the goats climb only one species of tree—the argan tree, which produces a small yellow fruit that is apparently delicious to hungry little goats. They stay with their feet planted firmly on the ground, eating the low-hanging fruit until there is no more and they must venture higher. Then, there is no stopping them.

You've probably heard of argan oil, which comes from this Moroccan fruit. I actually got to hold one of the baby goats and it had wonderfully silky, smooth hair—though I can't promise that can be attributed to the oil. I have used it on my own unruly hair, and it's good stuff. However, since I now know the original process for discovering and producing this oil, it's not so appealing.

The goats eat the yummy fruit, which contains a nut inside that is indigestible. Those nuts pass through the goat's system whole and come out the other end, softened by the trip. People first began discovering the benefits of argan oil by harvesting those tiny nuts out of the goat excrement and grinding them to extract the oil. If you're following me, you may have already thrown out your argan oil shampoo, but no worries, the industry has found new ways to process the oil. You aren't washing your hair in goat poop. But to be completely honest, if it guaranteed great hair days, I might do it anyway.

I am a journalist at heart, so as you can see, I ask a lot of questions, like who first decided to dig through the goat poop to see what they could find? And who was so curious that they rubbed it on their skin and hair to see what it would do? Whoever they were, I am glad they did.

Most of history's innovation stems from natural curiosity and a healthy sense of adventure. We owe much to people who chase a little wonder and think outside of the box, try new things, and don't allow their limited perspective or fears to stop them from attempting the impossible. Many of us owe silkier hair to those who were not thwarted by a little smelly goat poop.

My lessons learned from those tree-climbing goats:

- Where we see limitations, God sees possibilities.
- Adventure and innovation come from questioning the impossible.
- Don't be satisfied on the ground if God wants to take you higher.

- Sometimes you have to get your hands a little messy to discover the really good stuff.

Who knew I could learn so much from one very surprising experience with a tree full of goats? I realized I don't want to keep my feet safely on the ground if God wants to help me climb higher. I don't want to see only limitations where God sees possibility. I believe there are adventures waiting for me out there I don't want to miss, things for me to learn and experience, and even new discoveries that may benefit someone else. So, when it is tempting to say, "No, it's easier to keep my feet right here comfortably on the ground," instead I work up the adventure mentality that says, "Get up and try it! It worked for Pat; it may work for me." Every time I do, my life is a little richer.

This expectant mindset has led me to many amazing experiences. I've slept in grass huts, palaces, and the cramped sleeping berths of trains. Ridden elephants in Thailand, camels at the Pyramids of Giza, and donkeys to a desert oasis. I've been in planes that have landed on glaciers, grass runways in the African bush, the Amazon River, and that steep, remote mountainside in Papua New Guinea. I've climbed the ancient steps of the Great Wall, Machu Picchu, Masada, and Angkor Wat. Eaten wild boar in Tuscany, guinea pig in Peru, alligator in Brazil, and many other things about which I was afraid to ask. I've swam with sharks, held a sixteen-foot python, walked a giant cockroach on a leash, cuddled with a sloth, and slept with several uninvited giant spiders. And that only scratches the surface.

Some of you are reading this and saying, "Wow, I would love to do things like that!" Others of you are saying, "Wow, I'm so glad that's not me," and I get that too. Remember, God has a specific path for you, and it doesn't look like mine or anyone else's. But if, in reading this, there is something stirring in your heart—a desire to explore your own possibilities—now is the perfect time to begin. Don't procrastinate and miss something amazing…and most important, remember it is never too late. I don't care if you are sixteen and just getting started or if you are eighty and feel like there could be more adventure out there waiting; if you begin right now, I guarantee you things in your life will change. God is a God of promise and He will not fail you. In fact, He will blow your mind.

Are there times when I would rather sleep in my own bed and eat familiar food? Would it be easier to stay in one time zone and avoid the jet lag? Absolutely! And to be completely transparent, there are occasions when I am preparing to leave home and I just don't really feel like going; when I would rather do the comfortable thing and sit on the couch cuddling my puppy and watching Hallmark movies (don't judge). It's easier to stay cozy and safe, not too hot, not too cold, perfectly dry and secure. But inevitably, when I get out there and meet someone wonderful or see something amazing I never would have otherwise, I think,

"I wouldn't have missed this for the world!" Every single time I have been glad I got up off that couch, chased some wonder, and experienced life beyond the Hallmark Channel, in all of its messy, uncomfortable glory.

So, what gets me off that couch when I would rather stay put? That's when I must look past this moment and consider what I want for the future. So I ask you: Do you want a life that is always comfortable or one that is meaningful? Are you satisfied with the status quo of your day-to-day routine or do you dream of more? Somewhere along the line, someone may have said you couldn't do it, or it was impossible. Those are the people who would have said goats don't climb trees. They are wrong.

When I need a little push to get going and stir up my adventure mentality, it helps me to focus on those amazing rewards of stepping out rather than the ease of remaining static. I remember those moments I would not have wanted to miss for the world. So, let me ask you: How did you benefit the last time you stretched yourself beyond the norm? How good did it feel the last time you sacrificed your own momentary comfort to reach out to someone else? Are you willing to break free from the boredom and have an adventure?

PROTECTING YOUR TOES

By nature, we are programmed to play it safe. You know, "Safety first," and "If it ain't broke, don't fix it," and all of that. We tightly lace up our boots so we don't twist an ankle. We wear steel-toed shoes to protect our feet. I wonder, why are we so risk averse? Why are we so concerned about getting our toes stepped on? Of course, no one wants to be hurt, and we do need to protect ourselves from severe harm. We need to be wise and set healthy, protective boundaries. But when we avoid all risk and relegate ourselves to the safe and familiar, our adventures will be limited to living vicariously through *Game of Thrones* or *Dora the Explorer*.

If you don't risk twisting an ankle, you'll never come around a corner on a winding path to discover a beautiful clearing of wildflowers overlooking a spectacular mountain vista. If you are afraid to get your toes stepped on, you'll never drop your guard enough to connect with that person who may change your life, or you theirs. It's time to take off those comforting, protective, steel-toed boots that are keeping the world out and step into the wonderful unknown. After all, if you get your toes stepped on, you will survive.

So, what is keeping you from your next steps, from the beauty and purpose and wonder God has in store for you? Could it be:

- Your busy schedule
- Fear of the unknown
- Past hurt
- Insecurity
- Lack of motivation

This list could go on and on. I encourage you to ask yourself now and explore those things that may be holding you in place. As you do, remember that all of these things may be understandable but they are not insurmountable. We can become trapped by what others expect, by self-imposed limitations, even by our own success and comfort, or by our past, but today can be a new beginning for you. It is time to risk joy and pain, to allow yourself to make mistakes, to make room in your life for adventure, to learn, and to stand in awe.

Psalm 34:8 says, "Oh, taste and see that the LORD is good!" How will we ever know when we eat the same things day after day? Branch out, try something new, shrug off the impossible and reach for the unknown fruit at the top of the trees, then taste and see the goodness of the Lord.

STEP BY STEP

Defy the impossible! Instead of being chained down by those things holding you back, begin choosing:

- People over schedule
- Trust over fear
- Action over complacency
- Kindness over walls of protection
- Mercy over perfection
- Real over accolades
- Adventure over boredom
- Love over all

CHAPTER 3

INCONVENIENT AND MESSY

An adventure is only an inconvenience rightly
considered. An inconvenience is only
an adventure wrongly considered.
—G. K. Chesterton—

Our media team from Joyce Meyer Ministries had just arrived in Manaus, Brazil, and after hours of travel I was pretty tired. All I wanted was a shower, a bite of food, and to crawl into bed. In most countries we visit, we are hosted by the wonderful people our missions outreach, Hand of Hope, partners with in those areas to help people. We believe in combining our resources and skills with people in the field who know and love the region and their specific needs. It makes us both more effective, and together, we can accomplish much more. So, upon our arrival, our gracious hosts offered to grab a bite to eat with us in the hotel after we had a chance to freshen up. A kind gesture we didn't want to decline.

I don't know about you, but after extended travel the first thing I look forward to is brushing my teeth. Ahhhh. That toothbrush not only removes the airplane film from my teeth and freshens my sleep breath, but it also changes my entire outlook and generally acts as a defibrillator paddle, shocking my smile back to life. So, after a quick shower and a good brushing, I threw on jeans, a T-shirt, and some flip-flops—just enough to head back down to the lobby to meet everyone for a quick bite and then go directly back to the room and that beautiful, flat bed.

It seemed like a good plan but when I got downstairs, our hosts offered to take us to a favorite spot in town to eat. Okay, cool. After eating they mentioned a little detour to show us something fun. Now, you need to know I am the poster child for FOMO. My "fear of missing out" on something amazing, or much of anything at all for that matter, keeps me moving even when I am very tired. Part of me wants to say, "No thank you," but a bigger, more pushy part says, "What if this thing is exceptional and I miss it because I wanted to go to bed?! How lame could I be?" Some would call it a character flaw, and it definitely has gotten me into a little bit of trouble now and again, but it has also led to some of my favorite adventures. So, off we went.

This was my first visit to South America's Amazon, so I was

excited. Manaus is a bustling river city and the gateway to the surrounding rain forest. It sits at the confluence of two rivers, one blue and the other brown and muddy, creating an interesting phenomenon called the Meeting of Waters. The point where the rivers merge creates a visible line in the wide expanse of water; beautifully blue on one side and distinctively sandy on the other. These combined tributaries form the Amazon River. It is a fascinating sight.

As we drove, explored, and learned these amazing things, I was glad I was not resting in my room. I certainly would not want to miss this. Then, in a turn I did not expect, they asked, "Have you all been in the jungle yet? Let us take you to a really great spot." I immediately looked down at my feet and my flip-flops. Now, I may not have spent a lot of time in the Amazon at this point, but I have been in other jungles and have enough common sense to know you do not venture into the jungle in flip-flops.

Suddenly, FOMO reared its ugly head, or perhaps it was wisdom, I'm not actually sure which, but before I knew it, we were all walking down a path into the dense Amazon rain forest. It was just as I imagined: sunlight streaming through bright green plants with giant leaves larger than my entire body; beautiful species of trees with a network of roots and branches that created an elaborate labyrinth; and the strange calls of birds I had never before heard. Wonder was everywhere! And then there was the mud—the deep, thick mud.

As we walked farther, everything became even more beautiful and the mud even deeper. With each passing step, our feet sank just a bit more. Everyone knows misery loves company, so I'm not ashamed to say I was thrilled to see I was not the only one in flip-flops, not the only one whose feet were covered in a thick layer of mud. I began finding myself hoping it would work like a beauty treatment, leaving me exfoliated and silky smooth. I decided to consider this an unexpected Amazonian spa treatment of some sort. I squeezed my toes tightly so as not to lose a shoe and kept walking, crossing over tiny streams on downed trees like balance beams, exploring and enjoying myself immensely.

Then we saw it, a tree absolutely created for climbing, with huge branches stairstepped perfectly up to its top. It was practically calling out to us like a Kodak picture spot. A few of us instantly jumped at the opportunity, muddy flip-flops and all. Our guides carried a knife to cut back the dense foliage. I put it between my teeth and someone snapped my first Amazon photo in that tree—total Amazon princess warrior. It is still one of my favorites. Then we went back to the hotel, and I slept like a baby on that lovely bed.

Lessons learned trudging through the jungle:

- Don't allow inconvenience to interfere with an opportunity for adventure.
- Be prepared for anything.
- And when you aren't exactly prepared, try it anyway.

- I spend more time in trees than I realized.
- Life is messy.

Everyone reacts differently to being tired. Some get quiet while others get slaphappy. Our team travels together quite a bit, and we know each other well. It is a fantastic group, and I love traveling with these kind, funny, talented people. When we get tired, we have learned to understand when one needs space and another has crossed into that deep abyss of silliness. We extend a lot of grace. And they definitely extend a lot of grace to me. I'm one of those who get silly. For some reason everything just seems funnier, until you hit a wall and become the walking dead.

I was tired when we arrived at the hotel, so I could have easily said no thank you. I love to sleep—it's one of my superpowers. I can sleep anywhere at any time, which won't save the planet from an oncoming meteorite but is a huge blessing when you travel. But I'm so glad I chose to push through to my second wind…or was it my third? Good things often come with your second wind. As the saying goes, "You can sleep when you die." Of course, that's just nuts, so please don't go overboard. You need your rest to stay healthy and coherent. But I have set my mind to push through and, at least when possible, refuse to allow inconveniences like being a bit tired, hungry, or wearing the wrong shoes to keep me from something new. To chase that elusive wonder. That's an adventure mentality.

THOSE INCONVENIENT LITTLE FOXES

Inconvenience is the enemy of many great things. It sneaks in like an insidious troll and can stop your progress dead in its tracks—if you allow it. It says, "It's just too much work. It's not worth the effort. It would be so much easier to pass this time." Then, before you know it, "this time" has become nearly every time and you have missed out on life. Like the little foxes talked about in Song of Solomon 2:15, these small menaces come in and spoil the vine or destroy the good God has in mind for us. If I am going to overcome potentially serious obstacles, and I am determined with God's help to do just that, I have to begin by shutting down the little inconveniences that thwart my progress.

It was certainly inconvenient to be in flip-flops for this particular outing, but it was not a deal breaker. We were very careful, we watched where we were walking, and didn't walk so far as to hurt our feet. It wasn't ideal by any stretch of the imagination but more than anything, it was just messy.

Most of us work very hard to avoid messy. I know I do. I like order and organization. Avoiding a mess is a logical practice, but I have to ask: What do we miss out on when we shy away from a little disorder? Life is messy. An adventurous life is definitely messy. And I believe in order to live the purposeful, fulfilling life we all want, we have to get a little messy sometimes. An adventure mentality says, "I am going to risk the messiness of my plans not going exactly as expected, circumstances not always firmly in my control, and relationships that aren't perfect, because the return on investment is so much greater than the sacrifice." The bottom line is, do you want perfection, or do you want passion?

Perhaps the key is to be like a Boy Scout—always prepared—and when that fails, be willing to adapt. When an opportunity comes your way that doesn't line up perfectly with your plans or expectations, at least give it a second look. It could be the diversion, or the miracle, that you actually need. Be interruptible! God loves the element of surprise so leave room for Him to show you some wonder.

There are many inconveniences in life. One day, I was emptying the dishwasher when my arm brushed across the damp counter, sending a few utensils cascading to the ground. One of those was a fork that flew off the counter, tines down, and directly into my toe. Ouch! I jumped back and was grumbling about that stupid fork when I noticed something that abruptly shifted my attention: there was a very large knife stuck blade down into the hardwood floor, and it was right where my foot had just been. Got the picture? The fork that fell first, jabbing my toe and inspiring me to move quickly, spared my foot from the huge knife that was coming right behind it. One was an inconvenience, the other would have been a real problem.

I love to tell that story because it's a great example of how we complain about life's inconveniences, sometimes completely unaware of how God uses them to move us to where He wants us.

A TIGER BY THE TAIL

Years ago, I was hosting a talk show on location at a large amusement park. This park had a wild animal show and my cohost, Bob Placie, and I were interviewing the big cat trainer and his full-grown tiger. We were standing next to the trainer who had this tiger on a chain at his side. Our production crew was also there, along with the park's public relations liaison. The trainer told us all to move slowly and calmly but there was no reason for concern.

I was loving this! It was a great shot, a new adventure, and the trainer appeared to have things under control. Or so I thought. Something caught the tiger's attention and he began to walk away. The trainer was no match for the cat's strength and the cat saw no reason to listen to what he was saying. The public relations liaison, a young woman probably in her twenties, jumped up to help. Lesson to be learned: Never jump up to help a trainer with his tiger.

The tiger pounced, grabbed her by the leg, pulled her to the ground, and bit into her ankle. Shocking, I know, but here is the truly crazy part: with blood oozing from her leg, that PR woman never lost a beat, telling us she was fine and there was nothing to worry about. Pulling the tiger by its chain and tail, they got it off her and pulled her away. As they were driving the woman away in a medical cart, she was still calling back to us about our next shooting locations. She was not going to allow a little inconvenience like a tiger attack get in her way.

You have to appreciate this woman's "the show must go on" attitude. She was a public relations rock star. But this is where I must mention wisdom and balance. Be reasonable. When God tells you to stay still, stay still. When He tells you to move, move. When you're bitten by a tiger, lie down. Know the difference between those little foxes and the carnivorous cats. Don't allow inconvenience to defeat your adventure mentality but don't let a tiger have it for dinner, either. Ask God for wisdom and He will give it to you. Trust God and you'll learn to trust yourself.

Our PR friend may not have used the best discernment. Perhaps in her desire to help, she disregarded her own safety and made a bad choice. Her day was certainly ruined and I'm confident she did it very differently the next time, but she sure had a great story to tell.

DO I HAVE A STORY TO TELL YOU!

Jesus told parables—or stories—to teach us, to hold His audience's attention, and to make His point hit home. Deep at my core, I believe in having a story to tell. That's why I have spent my life telling them. Over the thirty-plus years I have worked in television, I have compiled, produced, and told thousands of people's stories, sharing them through all types of media and even good old-fashioned face-to-face conversation. I have seen the absolute magic the right story yields, and this is what I have learned: Stories are powerful. They have the ability to influence people and change lives.

The Bible says in Revelation 12:11 that we overcome evil by the blood of Jesus and the word of our testimony—our story. When we encounter God's wonder, we should share it. So, it is logical that the more experience we have with Christ, the more stories we have to tell and the stronger, and more effective, we become at sharing who He is with others. And that is our greatest calling!

I want to have many stories to tell, and I hope you do too. Great stories mean we are more than just existing—we're wholeheartedly invested, living life to the fullest and successfully chasing wonder. We're experiencing God's grace, mercy, and character in deeper ways, bringing the Bible to life. You are creating your own stories every day. And sometimes it is the simple stories, not the earth-shattering miracles, that impact people the most. Those are the ones that make people think, "Hey, that could be me too!"

I have a lot of stories from my travels. I love to travel. In fact, if you ask me about my favorite things, you can expect a long list of "favorites" that I enjoy. But very high on the list I will always include exploring new places and seeing new things. I've had the great blessing of visiting every continent with the exception of Antarctica, and I hope to knock that off the list sometime soon. When I do, I will definitely tell you about it.

Some believe "adventure" and "travel" are synonymous. My

opinion is that travel is a perfect catalyst for adventure and provides you with many stories to share, but you don't have to travel to live a big, adventurous life. You can create your own stories every day, whatever adventure you choose to live.

During the COVID-19 pandemic, my travels, and everyone else's, came to a screeching halt. Were my adventures locked down in quarantine as well? It didn't take long to realize that in order to keep my adventure mentality alive and well, I needed to focus on other pathways to the wonder I craved. And I found myself to be quite successful. I found joy in reaching out to others, in writing, and in discovering new adventures right in my own hometown—all very socially distanced, of course. Yes, I'll admit I was longing to travel again, but I was reminded that there is no limit to the wonder we can find. Remember, this is about your mindset, not your location.

Travel may be just the spark plug your life needs, but whether you choose to go or stay home, whether you choose to live on the edge or stay safely behind the guardrails, your stories matter. If you choose to, you can live wonderful adventures without ever leaving your city. Chase the wonder around you, activate that adventure mentality, overcome those inconveniences, risk a little mess, and then share your stories!

STEP BY STEP

- Allow some messiness to interrupt your life.
- Shake off those inconveniences, stop making excuses, and say yes to your next adventure.
- Begin a list of the wonder you discover and tell someone about it. Share one of your stories today.
- Apply for a passport if you don't have one. You never know when you might need it.

CHAPTER 4

THE WONDER OF YOU

All of us have wonders hidden in our breasts,
only needing circumstances to evoke them.
—Charles Dickens—

I was running one day when I stepped just right on a large sharp rock. Actually, I stepped on it very wrong because my foot turned, and pain radiated up my leg. Of course, in my typical way, I shook it off and kept running, then walking, and eventually limping. Keeping it real, it wasn't entirely because of the rock. I'm an avid walker but I don't run for long without dropping back to my fast walking pace. I am not a runner. And after this little rock incident, I wouldn't be walking or running for a while.

Next thing I knew, I had pretty new "pictures" of the inside of my foot and a brand-new boot. This was not a pair of boots (which I would have greatly enjoyed). This was but one big, ugly walking boot. X-rays confirmed that the nasty little rock had broken a bone in my foot.

This boot cramped my style in multiple ways. Shoes are meant to come as a pair, like peanut butter and jelly or Captain Kirk and Mr. Spock. They just don't work as well as individuals. Attempting to make an outfit look good with one cute shoe and one massive, therapeutic walking boot was pretty much impossible. And if the one cute shoe didn't have the same size heel as the monstrosity on my other foot, forget about it. Teetering is never a good look. I basically gave up and stuck with one black bootie with the same heel height as that silly old walking boot for six weeks. It was fashion torture and should be against the Geneva Convention.

Perhaps more significant than the impact on my personal style was the change it brought to my lifestyle. I love walking and hiking. It's good exercise, I enjoy the time outdoors, and it is the perfect prayer time. I have the best conversations with my heavenly Father when walking. But for at least the next six weeks, there would be no long walks. And on top of it all, my adventure mentality was severely jolted. I felt like there was no chasing wonder or anything else with this monstrosity on my foot.

I was very surprised at how that boot changed the way I saw myself. I was an active person, an outdoors lover, an adventurer. Who was I without all these things? I got a little sad, which I rarely do, and that led to darker thinking and bigger questions. Would I really ever heal? Would I have to stop traveling, playing tennis, doing the things I enjoy most? They were ridiculous thoughts with no basis in reality, but thoughts nonetheless. I had been wounded and the boot was the physical representation of that wound. That boot was all I could see.

I had to adjust my thinking and I had to do it quickly. Rather than seeing the boot as something holding me back from the things I love, I began reminding myself that it was the tool that God was using to bring my healing. Instead of questioning if I would ever be the same, I began reading, speaking, and believing what God's Word says about me and my healing. And instead of thinking I wouldn't be myself if I couldn't do those things, I had to remember that I was whole in Christ with or without those abilities.

Some of you have more than just inconveniences coming between you and the life you want to live…you have wounds. Deep wounds that have changed the way you see yourself or limited your perception of what is possible for you. They may be the wounds of rejection, abuse, grief, or serious health issues. You too may need to adjust what you see and change the way you're thinking. It may take time and practice but try to focus on the truth of God's Word instead of whatever your big, ugly boot may be. Allow yourself to see past that one thing you are constantly staring at and set your adventure mentality free.

I am by no means claiming this is easy. In fact, let's keep it honest, it can be exceptionally difficult. It may be easier said than done but it can be done! Cling to hope as your lifeline. Instead of concentrating on your wound, think on these things:

- "He heals the brokenhearted and binds up their wounds" (Psalm 147:3).
- "By his wounds you have been healed" (1 Peter 2:24).
- "Bless the LORD, O my soul, and forget not all his benefits, who forgives all your iniquity, who heals all your diseases, who redeems your life from the pit, who crowns you with steadfast love and mercy, who satisfies you with good so that your youth is renewed like the eagle's" (Psalm 103:2–5).
- "How precious is your steadfast love, O God! The children of mankind take refuge in the shadow of your wings" (Psalm 36:7).

When I committed to focusing on the truth in the Bible rather than the obstacles I saw before me, that negative mindset began to change, and I learned a very valuable lesson. My adventures were not stopped by that wound, but they did shift. God still had plenty of wonder awaiting me, even though I had to learn to chase some of it differently than before. Just because one part of my body didn't work, I still had much to give God. I could write, I could encourage people, I could laugh with my friends, and I could enjoy the goodness of God in so many areas. My wound would heal, and so will yours, and in the meantime, your adventure mentality can live on. And if your life looks different after the healing than it did before, God will use that for your good too, and your adventures may be even greater.

I would love to tell you that when the time finally came for the boot to come off, I was bright, shiny, and new, and back to my old self, taking long walks with God and wearing fabulous shoes. Two shoes that matched, no less. But that is not how it went. When the boot came off, that old pain radiating up my leg came right back. You've got to be kidding me! After all that praying and believing in God's Word, after changing that nasty negative thinking and staying hopeful and positive, everything should have gone perfectly, right? Well, let me tell you, friend, it doesn't always work that way.

My healing wasn't complete. I needed more time for God to continue the healing work He was doing. I needed therapy to continue knitting together the bone and tissue and to strengthen the injured area. And most of all, I needed to persevere, to not give up. Oh, I wanted to be finished. In a big way, I wanted to be finished. I wanted to be back out there doing everything I used to do, and I wanted to be done with this healing process. But if I had given up then, I possibly would never have experienced complete healing and could have done even more damage than I had to begin with. Take the time, put in the work, get the help you need. Talk to someone, a friend or a counselor. Don't fall into the trap of believing that strength dictates you must do this alone. A far greater strength blooms from perseverance, growth, and faith.

Philippians 1:6 says that "he who began a good work in you will bring it to completion." As much as I wish we could, we can't rush God and we can't rush healing. But it will come, because that is what God promises, and He is not a man that He should lie (see Num. 23:19). In other words, men may be liars, but God is not. When He says it, you can count on it. Your wounds are not placeholders keeping you from good things. They are badges of honor showing all you have survived. They are the very things God will use to display His wonder, to bring you into your greatest adventures. And if you so choose, they are your stories to tell. So, whatever you do, don't give up on your healing; it is happening right now.

Even as I'm writing this, I've been going through a lot of really rough stuff. Really rough. In fact, this has been one of the most difficult years for our family that I can remember in a long time. We have faced life-and-death situations, grief, hardships, big change, and now my father is walking through cancer. It is very hard to see the people you love suffering. I pray and I trust God, but it is so tempting at times to look at other houses in our neighborhood and think, "Everything is good in that house." It feels like the world continues to spin when your heart is breaking, and it should somehow stop. These are the moments when keeping your focus on the truth of who God is and what His Word says matters most.

BEWARE OF GLASS SLIPPERS

While we are walking through times of healing, or anytime really, a very tempting pitfall is to compare our journey with someone else's. Let me tell you from experience that comparison never leads to anywhere good. "Why is my healing taking so long?" "Why is she accomplishing so much more than me?" "Why can't I be more like that?" We've discussed the fact that God has a totally different plan for you than He does for me or anyone else, but His adventure for each of us is still wonderful. When we compare, we will always find some way that we fall short. There will always be people out there doing greater things than we are—or at least they appear to be greater.

Be very leery of glass slippers. They look wonderfully sparkly and elegant when you see them on some other princess, but when you live in them, they aren't always what you think they're going to be. They crack and they make your feet sweaty, which causes them to fog up and leaves you with some nasty blisters. Remember, Cinderella may have gotten her Prince Charming, but she couldn't even keep those perfectly fitting shoes on her feet, and she had some of her own emotional healing to do thanks to her not-so-delightful stepmother and stepsisters. Comparison is so very dangerous because you can never look at someone else's life and see the entire picture in its reality.

Rajasthan in northern India is an absolutely mesmerizing place; the home of maharajas and maharanis, opulent palaces, spectacular cities of pink and blue, and the famous Taj Mahal. When I'm there I think this is a land of fairy tales, and I'm instantly drawn to the brightly colored, ornately decorated slippers for sale on many street corners. You know the ones, with their pointed toes curled up into the air like elf shoes; if you haven't been there, you've probably seen them in movies. Of course, the first time I saw them, I had to try them on. They were beautifully handcrafted and incredibly uncomfortable. Those curly toes were tight. I looked around and saw other people wearing them and thought if they could do it, I could too. I found a pair whose toes were only slightly less pointy and slid my foot inside. Not as bad…maybe I could make this work.

So off I went in my new shoes in all my tourist glory. The problem was, the longer I walked, the more my feet slid down into the pointy end of the shoes and the more cramped my toes became. Before long, my old shoes were back on my feet and my toes were thanking me. Eventually the Jasmine shoes joined my other travel treasures back home, never to be worn again.

Lessons learned from pointy shoes:

- When doing a lot of walking, choose form over fashion.
- If the shoes don't fit, don't wear them.
- There is no comparison; instead, be comfortable in your own shoes.
- Elves must actually have curly toes inside those crazy shoes.

Remember how all those women tried to force Cinderella's tiny glass slipper to fit their foot? It didn't work, and when we try to force someone else's life, or accomplishments, or adventures to fit us, it won't work either. It is best to be comfortable in your own shoes. You'll avoid blisters, walking funny, and a whole lot of heartache.

I have small feet. I like to think Cinderella's slipper would have fit me, but I know better. I would have shattered those crystal pumps dancing silly at the ball or tripping over something before midnight struck anyway. I wear a size six, which is perfect for finding great shoes, since that tends to be the display size. Fewer people need that size so you can find some really great deals. Of course, sometimes the opposite is true and because there are fewer pairs available, the shoes you want are already gone. Overall, it works in this shoe lover's favor. But philosophically, it leads me to a larger issue—I have small feet but some very big shoes to fill.

All my life, I have been blessed to be surrounded by amazing people who accomplish incredible things and set the bar very high. It is one of the greatest gifts I could have been given— everyday examples of living well. My father and my grandfather, both devoted men of God, made it completely natural for me to believe in a loving heavenly Father because I saw them exemplify His love every day. As great leaders in business and the church, they also taught me how to extend that love to others in my care.

I have been particularly impacted by strong women in my life who make the world around them a far better place and embody a sense of adventure. Amazing role models like my mom, an unstoppable force, a firecracker (she even gave birth to me on

July 4) with a huge heart. She taught me to be strong and fearless, yet loving above all else. I watched as she volunteered her time helping battered women. She would pick them up from dangerous situations, drive them to court dates, and support them in any way she could. She stood toe to toe with more than one furious husband or boyfriend and always held her ground. You don't mess with my mama.

One of my grandmothers stood five foot nothing but she was a powerhouse. She was a kindergarten teacher who gave generations of children a sense of value and an educational foundation that changed their lives. She retired decades ago and I still hear from people who are living examples of her legacy.

Another grandmother was a beautiful woman inside and out, who wasn't afraid to get her hands dirty. She taught me about art and gardening and compared them to planting seeds of joy in people's lives. Those seeds of kindness we plant always bloom into something beautiful. Oddly enough, she wasn't a blood relative at all. My mom's mother died when I was barely walking, and this amazing woman saw a family who needed her love. She freely gave it, changing all of our lives forever. (Take note: one spectacular way to chase a lot of wonder is to adopt a family in need of love.)

My boss of nearly eighteen years now is Bible teacher and best-selling author Joyce Meyer. She has helped millions of people around the world by sharing the truth of God's Word and her own story of healing after a childhood of sexual abuse. She began a worldwide missions outreach that is feeding the hungry, providing clean water, rescuing women and children from human trafficking, and sharing the unconditional love of Jesus every single day. I get to be a part of this amazing work, and I get to be a part of her life. She is much more than a boss—she is a friend and a mentor. I love laughing and talking about life with this woman who is exactly the same off stage as she is on.

Big shoes? Oh my, yes! As I'm sure you understand, if I worried about how I compared to these great women and attempted to fill the shoes of these giants it would basically leave me whimpering, curled up in a ball in the corner somewhere. I would be defeated before I began. (Though I will tell you, I do get a standing ovation many times when I speak to a crowd. Please ignore the fact that it's because I just introduced Joyce.) I'm so very happy I don't have to fill their shoes; I only have to fill mine. And I'm pretty good at that.

The very best way to show my love and appreciation for these women, who have imparted so much into my life, is not to try to *be* them and to emulate their God-given gifts and abilities, but to take all they have taught me and to live my own adventures to the fullest. I learn much from them and so many others, and then I do my very best to honor God and serve people however and wherever He calls me. I am grateful our adventures overlap but they are completely different, and each one is just as valuable as the next.

Are you tired of the cramped toes and blisters of wearing shoes that don't fit? It's time to learn to be comfortable in your own shoes. What about those constant comparisons that always leave you feeling like you come up short? Comparison is like putting on a pair of blinders; it has the ability to blind you to the wonder in your own life because you are concentrating on what you think you see in others. Let's all decide right here and now to let go of all of that. Those perfect Instagram lives are not all they seem to be. Let's refuse to live our lives based on how many "likes" we receive. God has great things in mind for *you*. Things for which He specifically created you, flaws and all. He has placed great wonder in you!

So, what do you say? Let's pinkie-swear and make a commitment together right now. We all walk through difficult times, and that's why we are better together than we are alone. But together means support, not comparison. There is enough love, and joy, and healing for all of us. So, here's the deal. As I walk through this difficult time, and you go through yours, whether it's now or later, let's promise this: We will trust God, and do good while we wait for that healing or answer we are seeking (see Psalm 37:3). We will put aside comparisons and live our own adventures. And we will keep that adventure mentality alive and well.

Next time you're tired and your feet hurt, your heart aches, and you don't feel like getting out of bed at all...when you're broken and just waiting for the other shoe to drop, remember

God has not abandoned you. He is working on your behalf even when you don't see it, and with Him, all things are possible. We are in this together! And you don't really want to be me, or your mom, or the next Joyce Meyer anyway. You are perfect in your own shoes, and with God's guidance, they will lead you to your own big and wonderful life.

STEP BY STEP

- Consider what your "walking boot" may be. What is clouding your vision? What wound can you begin thinking about differently?

- Thank God for healing you in this very moment. The scar left behind will be a reminder of what He's done for you, of your strength, and a badge of honor.

- Whose shoes are you trying to fill or fit into? Make a commitment to let go of that comparison.

- How can you best fill your own shoes? Decide how you can honor God through your own gifts and talents.

- Keep your eyes open for blessing. In the midst of my difficult year came one of our greatest blessings ever, our first grandchild, Elsie. Your blessings are coming, too!

- Recognize the wonder God put in you!

CHAPTER 5

LIVING DANGEROUSLY

Never let the fear of striking out get in your way.

—Babe Ruth—

Suddenly there were men coming from everywhere and I could see nothing but angry faces closing in around me. As the crowd grew, I felt smaller and more vulnerable. I was one woman in a mob of angry men who had been pushed to the brink, and I could feel the fear building up inside my belly. The thought crossed my mind, "I've got to get out of here."

Hold on. Before I tell you the rest of that story, let me tell you *why* I'm sharing it with you. I explained earlier that I am an avid walker but not much of a runner; however, there are a few things that get me running faster than you can say, "Just do it!" I'm a smart girl, so when I have been hurt in a situation before, experience says to hightail it and run the next time something or someone similar comes around. I've run from pain. I've run from rejection. And I avoid mean people anytime I can, primarily because they suck.

There are many things we run from. What about you? Maybe you have run from things like:

- Commitment
- Your past
- Change
- Failure
- Responsibility
- Love

The problem with running, as natural as it may seem, is it keeps us from experiencing all that life has for us. A life without risk is a life without real relationships, progress, passion, and certainly without adventure or wonder. And that, my friend, is no life at all.

At the heart of all things we run from is one common denominator—fear. We are afraid to be hurt again. We are afraid we will fail. At times we are even afraid to be hopeful.

Some people are more driven by fear than others. This can be partially attributed to how we are built, our DNA, our personalities. It is also part nurture, how we were raised, our experience. For instance, I'm not a naturally fearful person, I'm not a worrier, but we all face fear. Like most of us, I have experienced some frightening things and have learned a lot from them.

Back to that angry mob I began telling you about. At the height of the worldwide refugee crisis, our team was working in a refugee camp about an hour outside of Paris, France. The ministry I work for is active in several countries around the world, working together with different agencies to assist these refugees whose lives have been uprooted and shattered. Their stories are gut-wrenching.

As is the case everywhere we go, my crew's purpose was to gather stories. We document the great need and all that we are doing to help through Hand of Hope. The best way for people to realize they can make a difference is to put them in the midst of the problem and introduce them to the people impacted by it. When real people become more than just statistics or images in the news, we learn to live outside of our limited view and develop empathy. It is absolutely one of my greatest joys and honors to share their stories of tragedy and courage—I firmly believe the people we meet are God's greatest wonders.

As you can imagine, life in the refugee camp is desperate, and therefore, there is a very delicate balance of peace. These people have seen the worst of humanity. They are broken and angry. Still, most people we meet in the camps are lovely and are willing to do anything they can to get their lives back on track. They are incredibly grateful for our love and help. One of the most beautiful gifts

I ever received came from a family in a refugee camp in Greece—
I'll tell you about that in another chapter. But the ugly fact is that
desperate people at times resort to desperate measures, including
violence.

We had been giving away coats, clothing, and backpacks full
of basic necessities, like toiletries and books when three men
approached. They wanted to tell us about their situation. This
particular refugee camp was relatively large and predominantly
made up of Syrian and Iraqi refugees. One of the men was the
leader of a large group of Iraqi men forced to flee their country
without their families. Just the day before we had been working
with a similar group of men from Afghanistan who were living in
a Paris train station.

There is a security checkpoint entering the camp, but
inside, there is essentially no law. The men said that if we did
not tell their story, they would force us to leave. We agreed to
speak to their leader, and our videographer, Kelly McClure, stood
behind me with the camera. The man began telling me how the
media refuses to show what is happening and the world doesn't
care about their plight. The more he spoke, the angrier he got.
As he grew louder it became very noticeable he was drawing men
from every corner of the camp.

As their numbers grew, they crowded in more tightly and
became more agitated. The sea of men expanded until I could no
longer see the edges of the crowd or the rest of my team. I felt like

one tiny woman in the midst of tremendous chaos. And earlier that very week, there had been a riot at a similar refugee camp— a camp we had also visited. The thought ran through my head to turn and get out, an instinct unfamiliar to me. Like my mother, I stand my ground. But trapped in the center of this angry mob, I was growing more fearful.

I began praying—hard. "God, please help us. Keep us safe. Tell me what to do." Then I asked a question that changed everything. I asked him to tell us what he wanted the world to know. He thought about it briefly, quieted, and his disposition softened as he began speaking from his heart. As he did, the mob changed and the situation deescalated. You see, we were listening, nothing more…simply listening, and that meant something to them. Before long he had said his piece and the crowd disseminated. For just a moment I stood there in the aftermath wondering what had just happened; then I knew without a doubt that God had stepped in.

This was a frightening situation and similar to the one in which I got stuck in that old tree on the mountainside when I was eight years old; when it was all over and I could breathe again, I thought, "Wow, that was very scary and pretty amazing." Amazing primarily because I saw God in action, and partially because I learned some very important things.

Lessons I learned inside that angry mob:

- You don't have to bow to your natural tendencies.
- When in doubt, pray more; speak less.

- People want to be heard.
- Don't run until God says go.

I can't even express how very grateful I am that God led me to do two things: to ask that simple question and to listen in silence. My natural tendencies may have led me in a different direction. I'm not bent toward silence; I talk my way out, and my usual reaction to opinions with which I disagree is to argue. God is helping me with these things. Normally my fight-or-flight reaction says "Fight!", which absolutely would have been the wrong choice in this situation. Tempers were already at a fever pitch and absolutely did not need any added fuel.

The fact that, on this occasion, my instinct said "Flight!" probably gave me the necessary time for God to do what only He could do, rather than my usual MO of reacting to fix things on my own. That simple prayer, "God, tell me what to do," was key. He held me steady, kept me from running, both physically and emotionally, and kept me calmly invested in the conversation rather than being swept into the emotion of the chaos around me. I think that peace in the midst of fear changed the entire atmosphere.

Have you ever felt similarly in your own life? Like you are small and defenseless in a nasty situation quickly growing out of control. You are surrounded by the unknown and can see no way out. If so, take comfort in knowing that God sees far beyond our limited view. He has the bird's-eye view. When we see only chaos, He is in control. When we feel anxiety, He offers peace.

LIVING DANGEROUSLY

Again, we all face fear, but it is not the fear that defeats us, it is the running. Through the years I have experienced multiple situations where fear could have stopped me from work that needed to be done and the wonder I would witness. Cameras draw attention, and not always the positive kind. I've been detained by China's secret police, shot at in an inner-city housing project, threatened by pimps as we escorted young women out of a red-light district, and been in the center of more than one angry mob. But in each of these experiences, and others like them, I was where I was supposed to be, doing what I was supposed to be doing.

Bravery is an interesting thing. You can be brave even when you feel afraid. Fear can be an important indicator of danger; using wisdom in a given situation is bravery. For example, unless you are a first responder, you should not run into a burning building. Be smart, not reckless. But in order to live a fulfilled life, maintain an adventure mentality, and continue chasing the wonder in your midst, you must stop running away at the wrong times. Stop bowing to fear.

UP A RIVER WITHOUT A GUIDE

When you go whitewater rafting, you depend on a guide at the back of the raft to use their paddle as a rudder to steer and to tell everyone on board how and when to paddle. It is a very important role. They know the river. They know the holes and rocks and steep drops. They keep everyone calm and working together. They understand how the water moves and when the river gets rough, they guide you through the rapids. Or at least that's the plan.

The very first time I went whitewater rafting, we were somehow blessed with a guide who did not understand this concept of calm and working together. When we hit our first Class V rapids (rapids are categorized I to VI) she got flustered, began calling out conflicting orders, and eventually yelled, "We're all going to die!" It did not foster a great deal of confidence. If I could have run away at the time, I might have, but there is only one direction to go in a section of whitewater. The next thing we knew we hit a huge hole that bounced our panicked guide right out of the boat like a kernel of popcorn—pop! Suddenly there we were careening down the rapids without a guide!

Somehow we made it through and eventually the water grew calm once again. We pulled our soggy guide back into the raft. We knew there were more rapids ahead and continued, with very little faith in our leader. Thankfully, we survived the entire adventure. We even chose to go whitewater rafting many more times, including larger, rougher rivers—but with much better guides, of course.

That is a great mental picture of what fear feels like. It's like you are racing through imminent danger, completely out of control, absolutely on your own with no one at the helm, and the voice in your head is screaming, "We're all going to die!" In reality, this is a temporary situation and the waters will grow calm once again. Some people you put your faith in will let you down, but your ultimate guide will never be bounced out of that boat. God will not leave you. He will not fail you. You can depend on Him. He is forever there to help you remain calm, even in the Class VI rapids.

Do you feel like your raft is flailing uncontrollably? Is it difficult to trust because you're afraid of being disappointed once again? Don't allow fear to stop what may become your greatest progress. Do you sometimes run from relationships because you fear rejection? Perhaps it is time to take that risk. Is there something you can't stop thinking about doing, but you don't because you're afraid you could fail? It may be time to give it a shot anyway. Tell fear you will not live within its boundaries anymore. You are brave enough to face rejection and failure, and even if the result isn't what you had hoped for, you will move on, better for it, because the possibilities are far greater than the risk.

Now let's pause for just a minute because I care about you and don't want to set you up for a lifetime of disappointment. There is one thing of vital importance we need to address before you bravely step out. This is a key element to your long-term success.

You may boldly face all these fears and find you remain miserable because you are still running—running from God. Is there something in your past or in the back of your mind telling you that following God will be too difficult, or that it will take all the fun out of life? Is it perhaps saying you can't please Him so why even try? Or that God doesn't love you anyway? If so, you certainly aren't alone. Many people have felt the same, and given the chance, God has proven them wrong.

The Bible tells us His love is impossible to exaggerate. It is immeasurable. It is wondrous! Psalm 36:5 says, "Your steadfast love, O LORD, extends to the heavens, your faithfulness to the clouds." He loves you. He isn't looking at you with disappointment. He loves you so very much that He holds nothing back. He is the reason you can move forward in the face of fear.

The problem with a life of adventure without a relationship with God is you will have some great experiences, but you will always be chasing that next high. You'll never be satisfied. You will have temporary happiness but will miss the real peace, joy, and fulfillment only He can provide. It is God's presence in our lives that brings the true wonder of amazing adventures into focus in our everyday life. He fills a place in your life that nothing and no one else can. And without that, you will always be searching.

EMPTY ADVENTURES

You can't hide in or attempt to get fulfillment and value from your adventures alone. One of the wisest men who ever lived, King Solomon, describes this experience in Ecclesiastes 2:11. He said, "Then I considered all that my hands had done and the toil I had expended in doing it, and behold, all was vanity and a striving after wind, and there was nothing to be gained under the sun."

What a hopeless thought! Like trying to catch the wind. I'm sure most of us have felt that way at one time or another. But when you stop running from God, that changes and you get a great benefits package only He can offer.

You exchange:

- Fear for security
- Anxiety for peace
- Searching for fulfillment
- Ordinary for extraordinary
- Dissatisfaction for wonder

I told you in chapter 1 that the first step in our strategy is cultivating an adventure mentality that serves as the foundation for how you respond to life and recognize the wonder around you. Christ is the footer that this foundation must be built upon; otherwise, it will not stand over time. Fear and the heartaches of life can beat it into submission, leaving you hopeless and dissatisfied.

So, let me encourage you to choose this as your next adventure—take the risk of giving God a chance. I don't mean just going to church. I'm asking you to crack open the door to a relationship with God, who loves you more than you can ever imagine. Don't allow fear to hold you back. God is pursuing you; I can guarantee it. And He doesn't ask for perfection, He is asking for your heart. Begin this adventure by saying, "God,

I'm listening, please reveal Yourself to me. I'm not running any-more. I am yours." And if you want more help, you can go online to joycemeyer.org/howtoknowJesus. I promise, your experience with Jesus will be a remarkable one.

It is true I am encouraging you to do something dangerous today. This chase after wonder, this adventure mentality we have been talking about comes at a price. It may cost you a little rejec-tion, you may have to stand up to a few bullies, you may feel a little pain. And when you stop running from God, take the deci-sion seriously because there will be opposition. But I promise you, the benefits will outweigh the cost, the joy will outweigh the heartache, the love will outweigh the risk. There is no doubt, I am asking you to live a dangerous life—because it is the only kind worth living.

STEP BY STEP

Stop running *from* and begin running *toward*...

- Stop running from empty adventures and run toward a life of purpose.
- Stop running from rejection and run toward opportunities for real relationships.
- Stop running your mouth and listen more.
- Stop running in fear and stand your ground.
- Stop running from who you have always been and run toward who God desires to help you be.
- Stop running away and begin chasing the wonder God has for you.

Live dangerously!

SECTION II

LIVE IN WONDER

*Always be on the lookout
for the presence of wonder.*

—E. B. White—

CHAPTER 6

UNEXPECTED DISCOVERIES

He who can no longer pause to wonder
and stand rapt in awe, is as good as dead;
his eyes are closed.
—Albert Einstein—

Many of my very favorite days begin with lacing up my hiking boots. Some of these are days full of adventure—hiking, climbing, and exploring God's creation. My husband, Tim, and I love being out in nature and enjoy everything from the majesty of our national parks to the simplicity of a quiet walk in our neighborhood. We enjoy our time together whether it's simply walking and talking, or that moment of awe when, after a long hike, we come around that last bend in the trail to discover a spectacular view.

Other days I venture out into long, difficult hours of trudging through disaster areas, trash dumps, and slums all over the world, encountering people in the most heartbreaking situations and bringing them physical help and expressions of God's love. These are days spent in some of the most terrible places on earth, places where I find the greatest hardships you can imagine and also the deepest, most meaningful joy.

I've learned that whether on the mountaintops or in the lowest valleys, God is always near. His wonder can be found in very unexpected places. There is great joy in the beauty of God's creation, just as there is in bearing one another's burdens and lavishly sharing His love. There is wonder all around, everywhere, and I don't want to overlook it. The great adventure is in discovering it.

I am constantly amazed by the stunning beauty of God's creation, and by how much of it we miss. As I write this, I am facing windows that overlook the woods in our backyard and tonight's spectacular sunset. It is stunning, so peaceful, and I'm enjoying it immensely. It will last a few minutes and then it will be gone, but I am better for seeing it. I could have been writing furiously with my head buried in my laptop and ignored the entire light show. Or I could have been sitting in a chair facing the other direction, and again I would have missed God's amazing handiwork. We have to be purposefully on the lookout for beauty or we may not even notice it right before our eyes. What a sad thing that is.

Tim and I both travel internationally for work. I love it. Him, not so much. I am one of those odd people who enjoy even the mechanics of travel. I love airports, flying, and hotels. Weird, I know. The more Tim and I delve into why I love it and he doesn't, the more we realize our outlooks on travel are vastly different. I tell him about the interesting people we meet and the incredible things we see and experience. He tells me how he doesn't sleep well or have much time for sightseeing. We actually could trade stories because both are often true for me as well as him. Our experiences are similar in many ways and most people who travel for work likely share similar scenarios. The difference comes in our perspective.

Undoubtedly, no two journeys are exactly the same, but we do get to choose how we walk through those journeys. Will we focus on the lack of sleep which sometimes accompanies travel, or the interesting places we see and people we meet? Will we strive to get the work done so we can get back home or be on the lookout to take in and learn new things along the way? Are we biding time or chasing wonder?

As Tim and I discussed this more and began to dissect the differences in our perspectives, we came up with an idea. We have more time and ability to travel now that our little nest is empty, and we did not want to grow apart as many couples do. I love to go most anywhere, and he enjoys travel when we experience it together, so we decided to try something. We have each visited many countries of the world but there was so much beauty right here in the United States we hadn't seen, as crazy as that sounds.

So, several years ago, we began checking out America's national parks and today we are both completely enamored with them.

We have immensely enjoyed our adventures together, like hiking the heights of Angels Landing and the watery Narrows in Zion National Park. We've trudged through Washington's Hoh Rain Forest and scoured Olympic's majestic beaches and peaks. We've explored Rocky Mountain National Park's Trail Ridge Road, climbed Acadia's Beehive, and taken a small plane around Denali's spectacular summit. The list goes on and we have much more yet to explore together. My unquenchable thirst for wonder has rubbed off on Tim, and his love for planning and checklists... well, that hasn't exactly rubbed off on me, but his itch has definitely been scratched.

Perhaps best of all, we have been amazed at the majesty of God's astounding creation while spending important time together, which we will always cherish. Our little nest feels a bit less empty because of these new adventures. And the wonder we have soaked up, indescribable.

THE DREADED VACATION MODE

Tim and I have two lovely daughters who have grown into amazing young women. Since they were young, we have loved traveling together and have shared many adventures. There was, however, one element of travel none of us looked forward to—we all called it "vacation mode." When it was time for us to head out for our destination, Tim would get very...hmm, let's call it *singularly focused*. His single-minded purpose was to get us packed up and out that door, on the road, and into that beach house or wherever we were going on schedule. Boom!

I'm also very organized, so it all seemed good on the surface, that is until we ran into the inevitable obstacles. Unexpected roadblocks, delays, and diversions that would cause checklist and schedule snafus. Sometimes the girls and I were the obstacles, and Tim's vacation mode would rear its ugly head, sucking the fun out of our family vacay. Once we arrived at the destination, everything was great, vacation back on track—until it was time to head home. Vacation mode part deux. Gotta get there and git 'er done!

You can imagine how well that worked with me. I was all about taking time to enjoy the journey, spontaneity, smelling the roses, living in wonder, and all of that. So let's just say there were a few stressful moments. The good news is we all have countless wonderful memories from those trips together, and once again, I am happy to report some encouraging progress.

With these new adventures Tim and I have learned travel is not as much about *getting* somewhere as it is about *being* somewhere. We take our time and see the landmarks along the way, but I also respect Tim's plan, which helps us to prioritize and therefore have the time to see what we really want. It is all about compromise. Voilà! No more vacation mode! Okay, wait, I promised complete honesty...let's try again. Voilà! Vacation mode dialed back significantly.

If you are looking to explore and chase after all the amazing things you possibly can, get out there. See the nation. See the world. Travel is a great way to keep your eyes and heart open to wonder, but it is not the only way. The wonder of the everyday world is an adventure in itself. Let me encourage you to live in a state of wonder, wherever you are. It will not only bring the beauty around you into focus, but it will also brighten your days and shake up the monotony of life.

BABY STEPS

How do you train yourself to live in wonder every day when the world is moving at such a ferocious pace and there are so many distractions? I've been taking lessons from our grandbaby, Elsie. She is our first grandchild and we are absolutely smitten, head-over-heels in love! I could write an entire book about the wonder in this one little girl, but I won't do that right now.

As I watch Elsie grow and experience life around her, I am constantly reminded of the magic in the everyday. This whole big world is all new to her and she has so much to learn and discover. She is tasting new foods and it's such fun to watch as she decides if she likes the flavor or not, making the most adorable sour faces. She concentrates fiercely as she explores a new toy. She stops to listen when she hears music. She breaks into glorious giggles when her daddy does something silly like dancing for her. Her eyes light up when she sees her mommy.

I want to be like that. I want to wonder like a child does, to experience life and the things around me like it is the very first time, because when we do, everything changes. The familiar becomes new. We notice the detail we have overlooked perhaps thousands of times. And each day brings with it the potential to amaze.

Perhaps that is a part of what Jesus was saying in Matthew 18:2–4:

> And calling to him a child, he put him in the midst of them and said, "Truly, I say to you, unless you turn and become like children, you will never enter the kingdom of heaven. Whoever humbles himself like this child is the greatest in the kingdom of heaven."

He says that in order to spend eternity with Him in heaven, we must live humbly and have childlike faith. But could He also mean that in order to see the reflection of heaven here on earth, we must become like an innocent child, turning from our jadedness and opening our heart to the wonders He has for us?

I've been called childlike before and it probably wasn't meant to be a compliment, but I've decided that's what I want to be. Like a child, I'll stay curious and learn new things. I'll laugh hard and enjoy the silliness around me. I'll stand in awe of things I've seen a million times but still can't possibly comprehend. I won't think of myself too highly. And I'll light up each time I see the people I love.

Our diminutive *Star Wars* friend Yoda said it well: "Truly wonderful, the mind of a child is."

IT'S A GOOD THING

Take a look at Psalm 27:13. I find it exceptionally encouraging:

"I believe that I shall look upon the goodness of the LORD
in the land of the living!"

King David, who wrote this psalm, is saying we can actually see the goodness of God right here on earth while we are living, we don't have to wait until we get to heaven. His goodness includes His kindness, creativity, love, majesty, and wonder. But how can we see all that when the world today is so broken?

It is easy to be so overwhelmed by the mess our world is in that we are blind to the good around us. I understand this temptation. In the humanitarian aid work we do around the world at Joyce Meyer Ministries, I've seen horrendous things. I've held babies in my arms who are literally starving to death while their mothers can do nothing but wait for the suffering of these precious little ones to end. I've cried with women who have been used and abused as sex slaves. I've walked through factories full of children who are forced to work day and night. I've sat with families living in tents in a strange country because their homeland was destroyed by war. I know the world is full of pain and darkness. But even in the midst of all of that, I have seen wonder.

I have seen babies snatched from the arms of death and their mothers crying new tears of gratitude, women rescued and restored from the most unimaginable abuses, and children who once had no choice but to work in dangerous environments suddenly free to play and be kids for the first time. I've seen families start over and smile again. God doesn't want us to be blind to the pain of the world; if we are, we can't do anything to alleviate it. But He does want us to notice that where there is sorrow, He is waiting with hope. That is the greatest wonder I have ever seen.

Wonder thrives in unexpected places. Those days when I make my way to the mountaintop, I expect to see God's majesty. But when I keep my heart open and look for it, I am constantly overwhelmed by the light of God in the darkest places. A smile, a thank-you, an outright miracle. And children are the best examples. Even in the worst living conditions, their joyous response to kindness will melt the hardest of hearts. You can't tell me the world is void of such joy. I've seen it again and again. Some of my greatest joy has come through witnessing sorrow turned around.

Perhaps we can't understand true joy without experiencing the pain. But when we keep our eyes and minds set on Jesus, even in the most hopeless situations, hope will rise, and you will see it too.

There is wonder all around you, even in the most surprising places. God's hand is always moving, and His love leaves a trail of evidence everywhere it goes. Wherever you go, I encourage you to ask the question, "Where is the beauty here?" I've done this all over the world and I have never been disappointed. I see the smile of a child, a hand lifting another up, a tiny flower growing in filth…and each time I find it my eyes light up, my hope returns, and I stand in awe of God's goodness. I am amazed!

Psalm 106:20 says, "They exchanged the glory of God for the image of an ox that eats grass." Very literally this verse means people chose to worship an idol of an ox over the one, true, living God. But I believe, even today, we do our own modernized version of this. We are so wrapped up in the earthly that we are blind to the wonder of God. We exchange the glory of God for an image of the mundane.

If you are ready to step out toward your life of big adventures, chase after and live in wonder. Breathe in the goodness of God everywhere you go, even in the busyness of life. Be aware of the extraordinary, hidden within the ordinary. Henry David Thoreau said, "It's not what you look at that matters, it's what you see."

Commit to notice things like:

- A beautiful sunrise
- The kindness of a stranger
- A toddler's giggle
- A clear sky full of stars
- A delicate snowflake
- Puppy breath

- A warm cup of coffee
- A comforting hug

Living in wonder has become habit for me. I notice. And to be honest, I don't know if I could continue to do what I do otherwise. If you want to avoid burnout, develop a heart that chases after and delights in the wonder all around you. It is a surefire deterrent.

I make it a priority to take note when there is something exceptional. In the midst of the ordinary, when something extraordinary happens, I don't allow myself to glance past it or shrug it off as unimportant. Every day I am amazed at the things I get to do, the people I am blessed to know, the places God has brought me, and the love around me. And that is true whether I am climbing the steps of the Acropolis or sitting at home in my living room. I'm happy because there is wonder to be found all around me.

You too can live amazed, in awe of the wonder around you, but it doesn't just happen. You need a little creativity, and a commitment to seek His wonder. Chase after it with everything you have.

Psalm 40:5 says,

You have multiplied, O Lord my God, your wondrous deeds and your thoughts toward us; none can compare with you! I will proclaim and tell of them, yet they are more than can be told.

There is more wonder out there than you can possibly find in a lifetime, but think of all the amazing days you'll have looking for it! Such discoveries are what keep life from becoming stale and monotonous. Just when we feel buried in the boredom and monotony of life with only the same to look forward to, God amazes us with a special little nod, tailor-made for us, and keeps us on our toes. So, keep your eyes peeled for the next wonder coming ahead just around the bend.

STEP BY STEP

- Do you get caught up in "vacation mode" or "work mode" or "parent mode"? Consider how you can stop concentrating on *getting* somewhere and enjoy *being* where you are.

- Wherever you are, ask the question, "Where is the beauty here?"

- Make a list of things you particularly love and look for them wherever you go. You will begin to notice more of them than you realized were there before.

- Do something childlike. Rekindle that wide-eyed wonder.

- Search for the extraordinary hidden in the ordinary. Take note of at least one thing every day that you normally wouldn't have noticed and write it down.

- Look up. Literally. You'll miss many wonderful things if you're downtrodden, looking at the ground, or with your head buried in your work or a screen. It's time you hold that head high.

- If you don't see anything else, look outside of your circumstances and think of who God is and His immeasurable love for you! There is great wonder in worship.

CHAPTER 7

SWINGING FROM VINES

Swing your swing. Not a swing you saw on TV.
Not that swing you wish you had.
No, swing your swing. Capable of greatness.
Prized only by you. Perfect in its imperfection.
Swing your swing. I know, I did.
—Arnold Palmer—

D eep in the jungles of Peru, not far from the Amazon River, we came across one of the most massive trees I have ever seen with vast branches filling the sky and huge ropelike vines hanging down. A local told us that very tree was used as inspiration for the trees in the movie *Avatar*, but I can't verify the accuracy of that claim. Either way, it was colossal and so were its vines. They were screaming out for someone to swing from them, so one at a time, each of us stepped into a huge loop and went for it, swinging high in the air.

The time came around for my turn and I was enthusiastic. *This* was my Tarzan moment! I grabbed that vine, stepped as far back as I could, ran and swung with gusto. I went flying through the air and…well, let's just say it wasn't pretty. My foot slipped through the loop, one hand slipped off the vine and I was a tangled mess, swinging tail first and completely out of control. I looked less like Tarzan and more like Shia LaBeouf ridiculously swinging with the monkeys in the final Indiana Jones movie that should have never been made. It was humiliating. Everyone ran over, grabbed me as I swung by, and rescued me from my tangled, precarious perch. Ugh. So embarrassing!

Then, at that moment, I realized I had a decision to make. I could slink off into the thick jungle foliage, humiliated and hoping everyone would forget what they had just seen…or…I could try again. I could toss aside the stinging memory of my ridiculous display and go for it a second time. It would either be great fun, or an additional layer of humiliation, so I laid all my chips on fun and tried again. After all, no one who saw that would ever, EVER, forget it. And "I meant to do that" was not going to fly. So, this time I carefully sat my rear end in that loop and swung like a preschooler on the playground. I didn't care what it looked like, and I had a blast swinging from the massive Amazonian vine feeling like the singer Pink on her acrobatic silk at a concert.

Lessons learned hanging upside down on that vine:

- Swinging from a vine in the jungle is not as easy as it looks.
- It's better to laugh at yourself than to retreat in humiliation.
- Being embarrassed is not the end of the world.
- Friends who love you will still laugh at you, but it's not so bad.
- A failed adventure is still an adventure.

A little embarrassment is not the worst thing in the world. Missing out on a great adventure because of the fear of it is much worse. Allow yourself the gift of looking silly, free of the consequences of being self-conscious. Oh, my friends laughed, but they still loved me. Laugh at yourself and you won't mind nearly as much when others do too. Be silly and love it! You will find some real moments of wonder there.

One day our youngest daughter, Morgan, proudly walked into the room with aluminum foil crinkled around her head and molded up to a high point. She was maybe twelve years old and told us she was keeping the aliens from reading her thoughts. She was being silly, and we all thought it was pretty funny, so I offered her ten dollars to wear it to the mall and tell people what she was doing if they asked. I saw it as a great opportunity for her to learn that being embarrassed is not so bad; in fact, it can be pretty fun, and in this case, lucrative. She thought about it for about half a second and off to the mall we went. Many people stared, a few people asked, she told them that she was safe from alien brain probing and became ten dollars richer as a result. We still laugh together about her foil hat adventure.

This "swinging upside down from a rope, letting them see your weaknesses" lifestyle I'm talking about entails more than just embarrassment. It's about the true wonder of freedom. If you take this to heart and allow it to, this unashamed vulnerability can permeate much deeper into the core of who you are. And yes, I know about this from a lot of personal experience.

I hate to cry. I hate it. I'm not exactly sure why but I will do most anything to avoid doing it in front of someone else. I imagine it's because I like to think of myself as a strong person and tears make me feel weak. I don't see tears as a sign of weakness in other people; I actually believe that vulnerability, the courage to expose your true heart is a sign of strength. So why do I feel differently when it comes to my own tears? I said I don't know. Give me a break already and quit asking! (Sorry about that; sometimes I snap to avoid tears.)

It used to be easy. I'm not an emotional person so I've never been one to cry easily. That is until several years ago when I went and prayed a crazy prayer that changed things. (A word of advice: be careful what you pray.) You see, I love God with all my heart but I'm a very strong-willed person. If you are too, you may understand where I'm going here and how difficult this prayer was for me.

I'm happy with who God made me. I'm self-sufficient, a creative yet logical thinker who doesn't get my feelings hurt easily, and these are all good things. But I didn't want my self-sufficiency to get in the way of God's plan in my life. I didn't want my natural insensitivity to cause me to overlook the feelings of others. I wanted to be moved by God's Spirit, rather than be an immovable object. I wanted to truly see the wonder that God puts all around me, not glance past it. Does any of that resonate with you? So, I prayed that God would make me more sensitive…more sensitive to Him and to others.

I didn't completely understand the potential implications of this simple prayer, but I meant it with all my heart, and God began doing things I certainly did not expect. I began to feel the needs of other people in a new way, whether I had experienced those things personally before or not. I became more aware of the immense beauty around me, in nature, in music, and in people. The kind of awareness that would move me to tears during a live musical performance; that didn't allow me to make it through worship without truly experiencing the presence of God, or to pray for others without deep empathy and shedding tears for them.

Oh, at first, and sometimes still, to be honest, I was not pleased. When I was struck with an awesome awareness of God's great mercy and grace during worship like I had never felt before and tears began to stream down my face, I knew people were looking at me and deciding I had some great sin in my life that must be weighing heavily on me. I was overwhelmed by His love and all the while I hoped no one was looking. I got really good at the stealthy tear dab. You know, raise your hand high in praise and then subtly bump your face up against your sleeve to wipe away the evidence. Crying? Nothing to see here. And I'm also fairly certain there is mold or something in the church that I'm allergic to.

Slowly but surely, I began to understand the freedom of this gift God had given me. Over time I learned that this newfound connection to God's Spirit was far superior to my self-sufficiency and I began caring less about what people thought of me or my so-called strength. Today when I'm stopped in my tracks by something wondrous that I probably wouldn't have noticed before I feel a bit less silly and far more grateful. And this sensitivity I prayed for has led to a new kind of vulnerability with people. God has given me connections I never would have had otherwise. Vulnerability is a bridge that can span the gaps in our relationships.

I'm still not a crier. I'm that same annoyingly strong-willed person, but I have learned to force myself to drop my guard. Let people think what they will (oh, that's hard to say!). And every time I do, the benefits overwhelmingly outweigh the risks. Whether it is personal or professional, as a friend or as a leader, taking off that mask and sharing vulnerability leads to trust and open hearts.

IN YOUR UNDERWEAR IN PUBLIC

You've probably had that dream too. The one where you're wandering the halls of your high school in your underwear, unable to open your locker, and everyone is laughing at you. Perhaps your version of this annoying dream is slightly different, but you in your underwear in public is the common denominator. I've had this dream in many different forms and always wake up extremely relieved it was just a dream.

We come out of the womb buck naked but before long we are naturally concerned about being embarrassed, exposed, and vulnerable. Now, you won't like this question, but because we're friends, I'm going to ask: Are these things really so terrible?

I've worked in front of a television camera since I was twenty years old. I began while still in college reporting for a local news station covering exciting stories like jump rope marathons and earth-shattering exposés on the feral cat population. I cohosted a daily talk show for many years. I sold jewelry and coins on a home shopping channel, survived countless hours of telethons, covered elections, disasters, and the unforgettable tragedy of 9/11 live on air. I've done a little bit of everything and loved every minute. Now through that camera I'm honored to encourage people with the truth of God's Word and to travel the world sharing stories of need and of amazing people who overcome incredible odds.

I tell you this because through it all, I have learned that to be on television is to be vulnerable. You can't do what I do without feeling exposed, naked to everyone with an opinion and a social media account. I've made my share of mistakes, misspoken or said something someone disagrees with, and there is *always* someone there to see it. No hiding. There is a familiarity but also a distance. So many people feel completely comfortable—almost obligated—to share what they think about you: your work, your appearance, even your value. There I am walking those high school halls in my skivvies all over again.

Why do I keep doing it? Because the joys far outweigh the comments of people who revel in my bad hair days. I do it because I passionately believe in this mission I share, and because I have discovered the benefits of true vulnerability. I have made friends all over the world; some I have personally met and many I have not. They inspire me, encourage me, and share their lives with me. You see, vulnerability inspires vulnerability, it nurtures relationships, and it draws out wonder. You will not attract true wonder with fake bait.

I'm just who I am. Some people will be pleased, and others will not. Some will be exceptionally kind, and others will tell me everything they see wrong, but I decided long ago that I don't want to attempt to be anything I am not. It's far too much work keeping up that facade! I'm happy with who I am, and while God is always working to help me be more like Him, He loves me just this way too.

We like our lives to fit comfortably into the right boxes—to make the right statement—but one very important secret I have found hugely beneficial is to grant myself the permission to step completely out of those boxes, to kick off preconceived ideas of who I should be and experience the freedom of authenticity.

Are things like potential embarrassment and vulnerability really so terrible? I am suggesting you allow yourself the luxury of the unexpected, to step out of the ruts we all walk in day after day and see how your life and the lives of people around you will change when you stop attempting to make any statement about who you are and let others decide for themselves. Experience the adventure of living with:

- Vulnerability
- No masks
- No pretenses
- No one to impress
- True freedom

We all have a role to play in this world, but just think of the liberty you could enjoy if you weren't constrained by your concern of other people's perceptions of you. If you could live free of pretense, with no one to impress, no masks to hide your truest self…what could that look like? Just consider the adventures you could have if you never considered appearances.

In the Bible, Paul is another example of someone who was strong-willed and learned the benefits of vulnerability. He explains in 1 Corinthians 2:1–5:

And I, when I came to you, brothers, did not come proclaiming to you the testimony of God with lofty speech or wisdom. For I decided to know nothing among you except Jesus Christ and him crucified. And I was with you in weakness and in fear and much trembling, and my speech and my message were not in plausible words of wisdom, but in demonstration of the Spirit and of power, so that your faith might not rest in the wisdom of men but in the power of God.

Paul chose to set aside his own wisdom, which he was known to tout at times, and learned instead to allow God to speak more through his weakness.

If you aren't too afraid to let other people see your weaknesses, God can and will work through them. I am by no means saying it is easy. Do you ever find yourself saying things like, "I knew that," "That was my idea," or "I was just about to say that"? I know I do. We want people to think well of us. There are some pretty deep-rooted attitudes and thoughts I constantly battle:

- A self-protective instinct
- Defensiveness
- Wanting people to know what I know
- Continuing to explain
- Blame shifting
- Ugly, basic pride

Laying these things down could be just the next step to opening your heart to adventure and wonder like you never imagined possible. What does humility and vulnerability have to do with adventure, you ask? It's simple—I have discovered that the people I meet all over the world are my greatest adventures and avoiding these traps are keys to honestly connecting with them.

God has given me one of the greatest gifts I could have ever asked for—He has allowed me a glimpse into other people's hearts, to steward their stories. As an interviewer, I have always loved giving people a comfortable place to share their lives and thoughts. It is an honor and a great responsibility. I have learned that when I am vulnerable, raw, and authentic, others are too. And they trust me with their greatest treasures; they share what they have experienced, the desires of their hearts, the truth of who they are. Vulnerability reaps vulnerability and hearts are knitted together. They trust me to either share their stories with integrity and justice or to keep some things close to my heart and private.

A SPECIAL BOND

Perhaps this is best illustrated by introducing you to three of the bravest people I have ever met, two young men and one young woman who will forever hold a special place in my heart. The road to that bond took a lot of vulnerability on all our parts, and a supernatural kind of love. For decades, the people of northern Uganda suffered horrendous atrocities at the hand of warlord Joseph Kony and his Lord's Resistance Army (LRA). All war is horrific, but here it was particularly heinous. Entire communities were destroyed, people were tortured and mutilated, and perhaps cruelest of all, an estimated thirty thousand children were abducted, treated as sex slaves, and forced to take up arms and kill.

Hand of Hope was working in Gulu, Uganda, with children who had escaped Kony's terror. As you can imagine, for them it was a long, difficult road to recovery. In October 2008, I met David, George, and Flavia, three teenagers who had survived the unimaginable but not without deep physical and emotional wounds. Their lives were shattered, they were plagued with dreadful memories, and they were understandably hesitant to trust or forge new relationships. That first time we sat on the ground together, they were obviously uncomfortable, and the silence was deafening. Rather than beginning with questions for them, I asked God for help and then began by telling them about me, my family, and our daughters who were about their age. There is really no way to explain it, but as we began to get to know each other, God did something exceptionally beautiful, and they began pouring out their experiences to me in a way that only friends do.

David was abducted when he was nine years old. His initiation into the LRA consisted of dodging bullets from the guns of his captors. Once he proved his worth and had killed a Ugandan soldier, they still threatened to send him to kill his own parents. David was broken, brainwashed, and asked to do the unthinkable.

But David didn't have to kill them—the rebels did it for him so he wouldn't have anything to go home to.

David told me through tears that he didn't know how many people he was forced to kill, and his greatest struggle was forgiving himself. I'll never forget his words—especially haunting coming from someone so young: "I always thought about committing suicide because I have killed people and done so many wrong things. How can I forgive myself for all the things I have done? I am useless."

Flavia didn't remember how old she was when she was abducted, but it's a night she will never forget. When the rebels broke into her grandmother's house, she hid under her bed terrified. They soon found her, pulled her out by her legs, and dragged her outside to a group of girls whom they took to serve as sex slaves for the LRA. Flavia told me, "Life was so hard in the bush. If you cried, they would say, 'You must be thinking of home.' And then they would punish you. If I wanted to cry, I would go hide somewhere and then come back and pretend everything was okay.

"For me the hardest part was seeing all the killings. They would kill whenever they wanted to. One night we were walking and came upon a group of men. They were forced to dig their own graves. They killed them and buried them. Others were tied to trees and left to die." Tears streamed down Flavia's face and mine as she shared her story. Flavia told me she wanted to share her story with me because she felt safe and loved. I knew it was a love greater than my own that she felt.

George's facade was perhaps the most difficult to break through. He had experienced such unspeakable things. But at one point, I could see a difference in his eyes. His smile was no longer hiding his great pain, it was genuine. When he trusted and opened those floodgates, I knew he had offered me an incredible gift.

If I had any questions as to whether God had really done the miraculous and forged deep connections in the short time we had together, they were completely answered two years later when I had the opportunity to visit my three friends in Uganda once again. The moment I saw them, I knew God's love had done something amazing. Their beautiful broad smiles and tight hugs brought tears to all our eyes. These three broken children, whose innocence had been ripped from them, were now filled with joy and hope. What we felt during those first reunion hugs is difficult to express and their transformation was nothing short of miraculous.

David expressed it best: "Before, I was dead. My whole world was dead. I couldn't see anything, and I couldn't do anything, but God knew the plan He had for me. Now I can see what I couldn't see. I can imagine, what I couldn't imagine before."

I could see it for David, too. I could see it for George and for Flavia.

You will never get to the true core of another person until you shed your own armor of protection. I had to allow myself to hurt with them in order to celebrate with them.

Are you tired of feeling alone? Are the pretenses you're shouldering getting heavier and heavier? Are you ready to let your weaknesses show? You honestly have no one to impress.

MY MOST VULNERABLE

Let me tell you one final thing about living with vulnerability. The most vulnerable I've ever been, the most naked and completely unprepared I have ever felt, has also been my absolute greatest adventure—motherhood. Bringing those two little beautiful girls into the world and then loving and leading them through life is the most wonderful and frightening thing I have been asked to do. Acting like I knew what I was doing would have made no difference. Pretending I was more important than I am would have meant nothing to them. Through this journey, I have experienced a pure and all-encompassing kind of love made up of triumphs and failures.

Our daughters amaze me. They survived my failings to become beautiful young women, accomplishing incredible things. Teach your kids how to live adventurously. Encourage them, give them confidence but don't do everything for them. Don't take the reins completely out of their hands. Lead them toward an adventure mentality and teach them to chase after wonder.

As a parent, allow your children to see your faults, tell them you are sorry when you owe them an apology, show them you are strong not in yourself but because of Christ living in you. Learn with them, grow with them, love them through it all. And through your vulnerability, you will all learn what you are capable of. They will thank you for it and this adventure you share together will be the richest of them all.

STEP BY STEP

- Go be silly. Live a silly adventure, enjoy the wonder around you, and pay no attention to who is looking.
- Give yourself permission to cry. Cry it out. Cry for yourself, cry for others. Express yourself and don't even care if anyone sees you. Not all the time—this isn't a license to be a drama queen, but when it's from the heart, let those tears flow.
- If you dare, pray this prayer, "God, please make me more sensitive. Make me more sensitive to Your Spirit and to the needs of others."
- Spend your effort lifting someone else up, rather than yourself, and enjoy the great adventure of vulnerability and forming new and deeper relationships.

CHAPTER 8

FABULOUSLY UNCOMFORTABLE

Discomfort brings engagement and change.
Discomfort means you're doing something
that others were unlikely to do, because
they're hiding out in the comfortable zone.
—Seth Godin—

I was on the bottom bunk with the thin curtain pulled closed, but I could still see the occasional mouse skittering along the floor beneath me. The lights would flicker as we went through towns and villages. The constant rocking attempted to put me to sleep, but each time I was almost there the noise of squeaky brakes or loud passengers would startle me back to consciousness. We were on an overnight sleeper train in India. It was cramped and smelly and I loved every minute of this big adventure.

It was very much like you probably imagine the scene—*if* you multiply the sensory overload by a factor of ten. You may have seen photos of trains in India so full of people that they are hanging out of windows and standing on the top of the cars. In the train stations people don't believe in queuing or waiting in line so it is total pandemonium. Everyone for themselves. You have to stand your ground or be pushed aside, which is difficult for polite people like us. When you finally get aboard and find your bunk, there is likely a family already planted there, and you must ask them to leave. They agreeably move on; it is just their way and they figure it was worth a try.

The thin, hard bunks are stacked two or even three high. They aren't quite long enough for the average person, but I sleep curled up in a ball, so it wasn't as much of an issue for me as it was for others. (Remember, sleeping is my superpower, though my abilities were stretched this time.) There is a thin curtain between you and the hallway, and when people walk past, the breeze they create blows it around.

Heaven forbid you should have to go to the bathroom. The toilets aren't…shall we say, very welcoming. Be sure to bring your own toilet paper, hand wipes, and sanitizer. Oh, and those are the nice toilets. Others are squatty potties, which are often just holes in the floor where you can see the tracks speeding by beneath you. I miraculously held it for hours!

In spite of it all—the sleeplessness, cramped muscles, and attempts not to think about anything resembling rushing water—I was living the dream. It was an experience I would never forget. I was chasing after wonder in a big way, headed to a new place in a sleeper train right out of the movies. It was a very uncomfortable night but many of those loud passengers I told you about were people from my own team. We were having a blast! And we were on our way to meet and help people—to share Christ's love—an endeavor worth far more than a little discomfort and inconvenience.

Being uncomfortable is not always a bad thing. I submit that you will never enjoy the big, full life you desire deep down without allowing yourself to be uncomfortable at times. You have to be uncomfortable now and then to experience some of your greatest adventures, to get where you need to go, and to truly explore your potential. It's when we are uncomfortable that we stretch, learn, and grow. It's when we allow a little discomfort in our lives that we discover wonderful new things about the world and about ourselves.

Without a willingness to be uncomfortable, we will never:

- Accept the challenge to try something new
- Dream about the impossible
- Risk failure
- Break free from routine
- Conquer the "what ifs"
- Learn to truly laugh at ourselves
- Witness the miraculous

I seriously appreciate a comfortable hotel bed with a big, cozy down comforter and lots of squishy pillows, but if I hadn't ventured out uncomfortably for many hours on insanely bumpy dirt roads, and then continued beyond where there were no roads at all to sleep in a hot, dusty tent and shower under a bag of water, I never would have experienced the incredible Tanzanian bush. I would have missed the wonder of knowing an amazing group of children who were once in such desperate need of water that their tribes were killing one another to get it. I couldn't have sat with them under the shade of an acacia tree and laughed with them as they played with my hair. I wouldn't have been able to hear about how much they love the school they can now attend because of a freshwater well we built in their village, sparing them hours of walking every day.

If I hadn't gotten seasick on a junk in Hong Kong's Victoria Harbor, picked up parasites in Egypt, gotten hopelessly lost in Jakarta, spent a lot of time in prisons (serving people, not time)— if I hadn't gotten uncomfortable doing all of these things, I would have missed some incredible adventures, opportunities to learn, to help people, and to experience many extraordinary moments of wonder.

Don't misunderstand me. I'm not saying I enjoyed all those crazy discomforts; I certainly didn't. But they were a part of the whole experience that I would not have wanted to miss. I could have reasonably chosen a soft bed, a good meal, and reduced risk of illness and injury, and you can too. But when I said yes to a bit of discomfort and inconvenience, I gained more than I realized was possible. I experienced deeper joy, love, fulfillment, and more life than most people ever get to soak up.

Don't worry, you don't have to get lost, pick up parasites, or go to prison; your adventures are different than mine. But if you want greater joy, love, and fulfillment in your life…if you want to accomplish more and live more fully than you perhaps ever imagined, you must be willing to set aside a little comfort.

Are you willing to be uncomfortable? This is an important question because life—real life—is not only about feeling good and seeing perfect things. The adventures that add meaning to your life don't always feel good in the process. But if you are willing to take it all in—the pleasant and the unpleasant, the good and the bad, the easy and the difficult, the ugly and the beautiful—you will go much deeper than the average person. This is where you see the real wonder. This is where you experience the miraculous. This is where God blows you away.

Comfort has become one of our greatest stumbling blocks. It keeps us fat, happy, and oblivious to what we are missing. It's like a drug. Think about it like this: You find that perfectly cozy, worn-in robe that feels like a great big hug each time you wear it. It feels better than anything else you wear. In time you get so accustomed to being perfectly snuggly that you refuse to take it off. It is comfortable but limiting. It isn't appropriate for most occasions, so you don't go. People begin looking at you funny, so you stay home most of the time. It certainly isn't part of your work dress code, and eventually, you lose your job. You are comfortable but you are missing life. In fact, you can't call it much of a life at all.

There is nothing wrong with comfort in general, we all prefer to be comfortable; I know I do. We shouldn't feel guilty about creature comforts and conveniences of life, but too much of even a *good thing* makes our world smaller.

Throughout the Bible, God called people to discomfort. He asked Moses to lead the Israelites out of captivity when Moses had no idea how to be a leader. He asked Noah to build an ark while everyone laughed. He asked Queen Esther to risk her life to save her people. He asked Jonah to go somewhere he didn't want to go. There really is no getting away from it. *Real life* gets messy and uncomfortable at times, so perhaps we should stop fighting it.

True wonder often comes at a price. Many of the most beautiful things I have ever experienced required some discomfort to get there. Early morning starts, sore muscles, and achy feet from hiking to the highest overlook are easily overshadowed by the absolute majesty at the top of that mountain. The hard conversations and tears you shed are exceedingly worth it when that relationship with someone you love grows stronger. Years of sacrifice pay off when you finally reach that goal. Those are the moments when you allow yourself to be totally overwhelmed by the goodness and handiwork of God and when you know you would do it all over again!

I recently went paragliding for the first time. Essentially you cinch up in a harness connected to a large sail called a wing and you run off the edge of a cliff. This was a tandem paraglide—I'm not dumb enough to run off a cliff without being securely fastened to someone who knows what they are doing! Yes, I know, some of you are laughing right now, thinking you have to be a little bit stupid to run off a cliff at all, but let's put that aside for now.

From the first time I saw people gliding through the sky high above the cliffs and ocean below, I knew I wanted to do it too. It was a beautiful sight, with the colorful sails against the crisp blue sky. I could only imagine how amazing the view would be from above and how freeing the experience must feel.

When I finally had the opportunity, it began with paperwork. Many pages of paperwork. I signed and initialed page after page acknowledging there was the potential of something going wrong and agreeing not to sue anyone if it did. It definitely made me think. Talk about uncomfortable.

Eventually the time came. I stepped into the harness and the instructor cinched it up high and tight, which was not exactly comfortable either. Hello, wedgie. Then he hooked me to his harness and instructed me to move when and where he told me. It was a lot like a three-legged race, trying to coordinate our steps while he wrangled a nearly thirty-foot wing above us. He said go and we ran toward the edge of the three-hundred-foot cliff. Goodbye to any semblance of comfort.

Then it happened. The wind coming off the ocean met the

cliff wall and was forced straight up. It caught our sail and lifted us off the ground! It was exhilarating and breathtaking. Suddenly all that discomfort was forgotten, and I was giggling like a kid as we sailed, relishing the stunning scenery and enjoying the freedom of gliding effortlessly through the air. He swung us back and forth, playing with the wind and adding a bit more excitement to our adventure. I loved it! The sky was crystal clear, the ocean waves beneath us were rolling effortlessly, and we were having a glorious time.

When it was almost time to land, a different kind of wave hit me—a wave of nausea. Evidently, we did one too many loop the loops and that old discomfort was back again. Time to get my feet on solid ground.

We landed soft, like stepping down from a cloud, and it was over. I couldn't wait to tell my watching family all about it. I didn't care at all about those moments of discomfort. I didn't even care that I was nauseous for the next hour or so. I had chased and caught a whole lot of wonder that day. I had done and seen things I never had before, taken in God's beautiful handiwork from a new vantage point, and I had a new story to tell. None of it would have happened without that discomfort and I wouldn't have traded it for anything. Although I was very grateful for a little ginger ale to settle my stomach.

Now remember, your adventures don't have to be the same as mine or anyone else's, but we have all had times we felt like we were out of control and running toward a cliff. In those times we have little choice but to endure the discomfort, trust in God who is holding on to us, and see where He takes us. If at all possible, sit back and enjoy the ride. The discomfort will eventually fade into the background and the wonder of His plan will overshadow it all.

Stretch yourself here and there. You'll see that fabulously uncomfortable beats comfortably bored every time.

STEP BY STEP

- Is there a strong desire in your heart you just can't shake but you've been avoiding because doing it will be uncomfortable? Make a plan and go for it.
- Choose one thing that is physically or emotionally outside of your comfort zone and give it a try.
- What conversation are you avoiding because it will be uncomfortable? Pray about it first, then go and talk it out.
- Don't let those uncomfortable circumstances or feelings pull you out of the wonder around you—stay in the moment.
- Even though it may be uncomfortable, risk that adventure while you still have the fire in your belly. The window of opportunity may pass, leaving you with the discomfort of regret.

CHAPTER 9

DANCING INTO CREATIVITY

Think left and think right and think low and think high.
Oh, the thinks you can think up if only you try!
—Dr. Seuss—

Hidden high up in the snowcapped Himalayan Mountains of Tibet, there is an amazing little town aptly named Shangri-La. There, Tibetans sell big furry hats and yak meat snacks. (I wrote that line with Dr. Seuss in mind.) In the distance, a long stairway climbs to a large, colorful monastery with golden domes overlooking the village. It is quite picturesque and quite cold. When we were there, it was exactly like I had imagined Tibet, drenched in snow and freezing cold. I have *never* been so cold.

Our visit was several years ago and I'm sure times have changed a bit for Shangri-La. The name itself draws some tourists, and the town has likely adapted accordingly, but when we visited, there were few amenities and there was very little to do. There was a great deal of snow, a lot of yaks, and no Wi-Fi or cell service.

But each evening when the sun went down, something truly wonderful happened. Something the likes of which I have never seen before or since. The people came out of their homes into the open-air town square and they danced. They bundled up with as little exposed skin as possible, flooded the tiny square, played traditional instruments, and danced. It was a sight to behold! It didn't last exceptionally long, it was too cold for that, but when we were there, they openly welcomed us into their circle and we danced together. For those magnificent minutes we were no longer outsiders, everyone forgot about how cold they were, and the square was filled with music and ear-to-ear smiles as we all shared a Tibetan folk dance. It was magical!

Lessons I learned in that Tibetan town square:

- Yak hats are delightfully warm.
- More people around you equals more warmth for your body and your heart.
- You can stay bored, or you can get creative.
- Sometimes, you just need to dance.

Studies, including the General Social Survey[1] and the World Happiness Report,[2] show overall happiness in America is on the decline and has been for several years. Boredom and dissatisfaction with life in general is a growing problem. Considering how busy and overscheduled we all are, how many things we have to check off our to-do lists, and the fast-and-furious pace at which we live, boredom seems impossible; yet we often say we feel trapped in the monotony of it all. Perhaps monotony is precisely why we are bored, even in our rushing about.

When I think of the people of Shangri-La, I am struck by those things that could render their lives "boring"—the remote location, the climate, and lack of entertainment options like cinema multiplexes or even a Target. I'm sure they had things to check off their lists too, and I know it was warmer in their homes than it was outside, yet they were savvy enough to know what they needed most. They got out and purposefully chased a little wonder. They sought human interaction—no matter how cold it was out there. They didn't sit night after night, prisoners of circumstance and the elements; they got creative and found a way to break the tedium of routine. And I must say, what they did was wonderfully creative.

My title at Joyce Meyer Ministries is chief creative officer, so I firmly believe in creativity. It isn't just about bells and whistles; creativity is necessary and meaningful. It is a key component to keeping any project from becoming noise and disappearing into oblivion, and it's a key component for life, keeping us from fading into the noise around us as well. Creativity is what rescues us from boredom and sparks new adventures.

If you don't want to live bored, you have to get creative and break the mold of routine. If you feel stifled, like your adventure gene is turned off, you have to break out of that box so many people have put you in—your parents, friends, boss—or perhaps you nailed that lid on all by yourself. If you'll begin to view each day as a fresh opportunity to experience wonder rather than to simply fulfill obligations, and begin incorporating a little creativity, adventure comes alive.

You may or may not think of yourself as a creative, but I believe everyone has creativity inside of them, especially those of us who walk with God and have His Holy Spirit to help us. Remember Jeremiah 33:3? "Call to me and I will answer you, and will tell you great and hidden things that you have not known."

That, my friend, is the perfect recipe for creativity. God is the great Creator and He is willing to share His ideas with us; all we have to do is ask. We need inspiration. So don't just seek to be creative, seek to be inspired. Seek to be led by the Creator of all!

You may have preconceived ideas of creativity or a creative process that are holding you back. You don't have to be a Picasso or Salvador Dalí; you can enjoy your own brand of creativity. For me, creativity comes in many different packages. I appreciate an organized process, but I don't always want complete structure or symmetry. I love the unexpected. You may be a messy creative whose ideas come out of random inspiration, or a buttoned-down, by-the-book type who gets just a little jazzed by new ideas at times. Whatever sparks your imagination, be creative enough not to be constrained by other people's ideas of how it should work. Step into creativity and see where it leads you. The wonder you discover may surprise you.

IT ONLY TAKES A SPARK

Some of you are already all over this and are right now thinking up creative ways to head out on your next adventure and spice up your life. But for you, my friend, who is still not sure if you have a creative bone in your body, fear not! I believe in you, and together, we are going to wake up your inner da Vinci. And face it, even you creative geniuses in full bloom may need a little fresh inspiration.

First of all, you must make time for creativity. A creative thought might drop out of a tree and hit you on the head, like that apple hit Isaac Newton, but it's unlikely. You need some time outside of the day-to-day treadmill of routine to think. Build in margin for the unexpected; make room in your life to stand in awe and chase a little inspiration. The people of Shangri-La scheduled a time every night to go outside, clear their heads, and dance. You've got to dance. Make it a priority and just go for it!

What is your passion? When you allow yourself to put time and energy into something you love, everything becomes an adventure. When I'm working on a project I'm passionate about, I often can't stop thinking about it. Not because I'm obsessed or under the pressure of a deadline, but because I love it. I'm excited about it and new thoughts just keep coming. When I'm brushing my teeth or taking a shower, and I get an out-of-thin-air idea or sudden clarity, I am sure to immediately jot it down so I don't lose the inspiration. I keep my phone or a notepad by my bed so I can clear my head of the thoughts that continue to come as I'm winding down for the night, and once those are out, I sleep like a baby. Discover your passion and you may discover your creativity.

What are your talents? God has put amazing things inside each one of us, and that means you too. I can guarantee it. When you give yourself permission and time to explore your talents, whether you use them in your day-to-day work or not, you will be more productive and creativity will flow. Are you a musician, a cook, or an organizer? Are you great with numbers, or kids, or are you a leader of people? There is creativity in all those things. Find an outlet for your talent and you will be less bored and more satisfied because you are feeding the gifts God has placed in you. But don't just think of the typical roles or opportunities; allow yourself to dream outside of that box.

Let go of your fear of failure. Creativity can only flourish in a safe environment, an environment where risks are taken because failure doesn't mean final. I look at creativity like some describe love: release it and if it comes back to you, it is a success; if it doesn't, it was worth a try. I am blessed to work in an environment where we are free to try and sometimes fail. You can't be creative and perfect. Allow yourself permission to try and fail sometimes. It's not the end of the world and may be the beginning of something beautiful.

Do something you would never do. Break out of the mundane and do something completely different. It can open new doors for the wonder you are seeking and spark creativity you would have never found otherwise.

I'm an animal lover through and through. All my life I have been rescuing injured and abandoned critters. One day my mom opened the glass doors that covered our fireplace and discovered it was the new home to a nest of baby mice I had rescued. She was *not* happy. I've rescued bunnies, birds, cats, dogs, and turtles.

Needless to say, I am not a hunter. I'm not against others who are, but I am not. So, when new friends from an Amazonian tribe in Brazil invited a group of us to join them on a nighttime alligator hunt, the first words out of my mouth were, "No, thank you very much." I would have never in my wildest dreams imagined that this could be something I would do, but further consideration led me to realize it was an adventure I shouldn't turn down.

We went out into the pitch-black night with this group of hunters carrying their spears and handmade dugout canoes and looked for alligators. When we reached a pond on an island in the middle of the Amazon River, they told us to shine our flashlights across the water and we found them! Staring back at us through the darkness were dozens of pairs of red shining eyes. It was surreal, shocking, and quite amazing.

A couple of men went out in the canoe, speared an alligator, and dragged it back to the shore. In complete transparency, I looked away for the rest. Then they carried it back to their village and the next day we ate a delicious lunch of alligator meat. It was a night I will never forget!

Experiences like this fuel my creativity because they break me out of the ordinary. They remind me that every day does not have to be the same; that people live very different existences than I do, and there are seven billion different ways to look at things. Some days are meant to be extraordinary. I don't care if you go on an alligator hunt or visit your mother-in-law but do something you normally wouldn't do and gather some new inspiration for your creativity and your passion for life.

Here are a few more suggestions to kindle your creativity:

- Stay ever curious.
- Be playful.
- Say yes more than no.
- Listen longer.
- Embrace the unexpected.

Finally, be open to creativity in all aspects of life—don't relegate it to certain places or times. Fight the boredom and dissatisfaction that is plaguing so many by refusing to succumb to the tedium of living overscheduled, overworked, and unsatisfied. Be creative in your work, at home, with your kids, at church, in the bedroom (yes, I went there—and right after I said "at church," too).

The sun is setting and it's time to come out and dance. Flex your creative muscle and see what wonder it leads you to.

STEP BY STEP

- Stop these words before they slip past your lips:

    "I'm bored."

    "I'm not creative."

- Replace them with phrases like these:

    "I'm going to switch things up and…"

    "I've got an idea…"

- Explore how you can build margin into your schedule and give yourself the time to be creative.

- List your passions and talents; they are an important part of your creativity.

- Do something you normally wouldn't do—just keep it legal.

- Allow your creativity to flow without fear. You will fail at times, but you'll learn along the way.

CHAPTER 10

ENLARGING YOUR WORLD

I believe in being strong when everything seems to be going wrong. I believe that happy girls are the prettiest girls. I believe that tomorrow is another day, and I believe in miracles.
—Audrey Hepburn—

The world is a big place, but my question to you is, how large is your world? You do have influence over the size of your world. Does that surprise you? I have visited many countries, but that is only a small part of what makes my world large. Even if you are never able to leave your home, your world can still be big. On the other hand, you can travel the world and still live a very small life. It all depends on your sense of potential, expectation, and belief.

Do you believe in big possibilities?

One vacation when our daughter Taylor was young, she was playing on the beach and a wave caught her by surprise, sending her toppling. She came up laughing and was completely fine but noticeably missing her sandals—her very favorite pink flip-flops.

Our family loves our adventures together, and among our favorites are our times at the beach. Living adventurously requires variety. For me, that means having some times of bustling excitement, others of exploring new things, and some of glorious rest and refreshment. Through the years, our beach vacations have been beautiful times of connection, laughter, and relaxation. But this unexpected turn of events threatened to put a damper on our trip.

Taylor was not happy and we scoured the beach for her missing sandals. They were nowhere to be found and eventually we declared them lost at sea. She, however, was not giving up so easily. That night she made it clear that she had prayed and asked God to give her back her flip-flops. I'll be honest and tell you that in this situation, we did not have the faith she did.

Several days went by and we honestly weren't even considering the possibility of ever seeing those little pink shoes again. But when we were walking the beach, we saw something pink in the distance. No, it couldn't be. But it was! Lying in the sand in front of us quite a way down the beach from our rental was a small flip-flop. Okay, I understand that can happen, and finding one sandal may not exactly fit miracle criteria, but just wait. We picked up the shoe and as we continued walking, we saw another pink object—Taylor's other flip-flop. We found not one, but both! She had her pair of precious pink sandals back.

What do you think now? Still not sold? How about the fact that there had been many high tides since they were swept away, and even though we had walked the beach every day, they just now turned up? Or that no one else on the beach had picked them up? And here's the kicker: the current was pushing everything down the beach one way, but we found the shoes in the opposite direction. Can I get a "Hallelujah!" now?

There may be natural factors that came into play here involving cycles of the moon, ocean currents, or dolphin activity, but the point is God answered our little girl's prayer. I don't care how He chose to do it; Taylor was thrilled and knew without a doubt God had given her back her shoes. They became known as the miracle flip-flops, and her world became a little bit bigger.

This certainly isn't the most important thing anyone has ever asked of God, and I'm not sure why He chose to fulfill this particular request, but I do have a theory. I think God wanted to teach one little girl how very much He loves her, that He hears her, that prayer works, and that, yes, Taylor, miracles do happen. And all our faith was strengthened that day.

Belief, anticipation, and hope make our world much larger. And I love this flip-flop example because we often hold on to the misconception that miracles have to be earth-shattering...that wonder only comes in the extra-large size. Many of the miracles we experience are small wonders, the little things that never could have happened without God's hand leading them, and far too often those are the lovely gifts we overlook.

Sometimes our lives are so busy with the everyday activities of working, doing, and struggling that we forget to believe. When that happens, the borders close in on us. The routine monotony of the expected narrows our vision and our world becomes a small box. We stop chasing wonder because we don't believe there is enough out there. Belief in the improbable, faith for the impossible, even an expectation of the miraculous broadens your world because the scope of possibilities becomes endless and wonder comes to life.

I believe in miracles. I think most people of faith believe in the possibility of miracles, but do they believe they actually happen? Our God is a big, powerful God, but we keep Him small in our own world when we focus on the seemingly impossible and ignore the wonder and majesty that He is. Sometimes we just don't give Him credit where credit is due.

I believe in miracles because I have seen a few; some even greater than the miracle of the flip-flops (said with tongue firmly in cheek), and I believe in the miraculous all around us if we will only keep our eyes and hearts open to seeing it. The *Oxford* dictionary defines the word *miracle* as "a surprising and welcome event that is not explicable by natural or scientific laws and is therefore considered to be the work of a divine agency," "a highly improbable or extraordinary event, development, or accomplishment that brings very welcome consequences."[1]

If you consider these definitions, you may think of a miracle or two of your own. Open the lid to that box. There are surprises and extraordinary events that really can't be explained any other way. Some are wonderful little winks from God, while others are serious displays of His power.

A VERY UNEXPECTED WINK

Unexpected winks remind me of one morning in Sri Lanka when I saw a line of Buddhist monks walking along the road. The sight of this line of somber men in their long, orange robes was familiar. In the morning the monks walk through the streets and people offer them alms, usually gifts of food. But what happened this morning was quite unexpected. As they walked past us, one young monk in the center of the group turned, looked directly at me, and winked. Yeah, he winked at me! I was completely caught off guard and broke out giggling like a schoolgirl. He smiled a mischievous smile and continued walking in line with the others. The thought of that wink kept me laughing the rest of the day.

That hilarious wink reminded me of how very alike we all are deep down. I didn't expect that monk to have such a playful spirit. You may not see that you have a great deal in common with someone on the surface, then they may just turn and wink at you, changing all your misconceptions. I am so grateful for the joy that springs out of the completely unexpected.

I have also seen the impossible happen. I remember when our

doctor told us with tears in her eyes that our daughter Morgan, who was six years old at the time, had leukemia. Our world came crashing down. We were rushed to a larger children's hospital in another city and as my husband and I sat with her night after night in the pediatric cancer ward, many people were praying.

Then one day doctors came into the room perplexed and told us that there was no sign of cancer. Whether God took the cancer or the initial diagnosis was incorrect didn't matter to us. It was the miracle for which we had all been praying. We knew that God had healed our little girl.

Another time, as our team was working on a story about infant mortality in Malawi, we came across an outdoor market in a small village. Along the side of the road was a tiny wooden coffin that our driver-interpreter explained to us was part of the market and was there for purchase. With his help, we got out of the car to get a shot of the market and coffin to add to the story.

Suddenly, an angry mob approached. We discovered our interpreter had been incorrect; we had actually come across an infant's funeral that had been interrupted when a fight broke out among the crowd before we got there. They'd left the coffin on the side of the road and moved away as the argument intensified. When they returned and saw us, they were already agitated and became even more furious.

They forcibly took our interpreter and two of the guys on our team and demanded the rest of us wait in the car. A woman came to the window and warned us it would be very dangerous to get out. Our interpreter had the car keys and any available help was many miles away; we had no cell service and could do little but pray.

After what seemed like an eternity, we saw our friends walking back to the vehicle. The interpreter explained that the mob had decided to beat them. Then he was shocked when suddenly and without explanation, they stopped yelling and a calm came over them. The interpreter gave them the small amount of money he had, and they told our friends to go. Everyone was shaken but unscathed, and we drove away quickly, relieved and grateful for God's obvious protection and intervention.

Where there is no apparent way, God makes a way. I have seen the impossible on multiple occasions. I believe in miracles and nothing will ever convince me otherwise. Where there is prayer, where there is even a glimmer of faith, there is potential for anything. Honestly, if I didn't believe that, I couldn't do what I do. I would be so limited by my own abilities and expectations I likely would have never stepped into the adventures that have changed my life and others. Instead, I spend much of my life swept up in the wonder of all God is doing.

There have also been those times, of course, that I have faced terrible disappointment; occasions when prayer wasn't answered as I had hoped, and the miracle didn't come. There have been many personal heartbreaks, as well as days when the weight of our broken world just seemed too much to bear. Those are the most difficult days.

There was a young girl in Phnom Penh, Cambodia, named Ghi. Eight-year-old Ghi lived and worked in a trash dump, searching for anything that could bring her family a few cents.

The dump was a horrendous place, full of children who worked day and night, wearing small lights on their heads, dodging dangers like trash landslides, hypodermic needles, and huge dump trucks and bulldozers that moved in disregard of children beneath them. It was like a scene from a postapocalyptic movie. Our missions arm, Hand of Hope, had the brilliant idea to convert a bus into a traveling school where children like Ghi could get a good meal, a shower, clean clothes, learn to read and write, and hear about Jesus' love for them. It miraculously changed the lives of many children.

Sweet Ghi was shy, but she and I connected immediately. We made arrangements for her to go to the bus, giving her a real chance at a better life. A happy ending to our trip. But the next year when we returned to the trash dump and the bus, Ghi was nowhere to be found. We went to the makeshift house, a tiny shack on stilts at the edge of the dump where Ghi and her sister lived. I was thrilled to find her there. As we walked up, a beautiful smile of recognition lit up her face. But my joy was short-lived. I learned that even though all the arrangements had been made, Ghi's parents refused to allow her to go to the bus or attend classes.

Tears streamed down my face that evening as we left the dump. I have seen many horrendous situations but at that point I felt like

I had reached my limit. "Why, God? Why couldn't this work out for Ghi? What does the future hold for her now?"

Having faith doesn't mean you get everything you ask God for, and this really big world can also bring big heartache. But I would rather help as many people as I can and believe in the miraculous than quit trying because it doesn't always work out. I would rather hurt at times in a big world of potential than feel safe in a tiny world all my own.

There was another beautiful girl named Ababa in Angacha, Ethiopia. She wore a purple scarf and was terribly malnourished when her mother brought her to one of our feeding programs. She responded well to the nourishment and was growing stronger. I'll never forget her bright, beautiful smile.

Once again, when we made a return visit, we were anxious to see her, but on our way there, we got the devastating news that Ababa had just passed away. We were all heartbroken.

When we did get to the feeding program, I saw something that shocked me. There was Ababa's mother with a little girl in the same purple scarf. Could it be? Was our information incorrect? Then I realized this child was Ababa's baby sister. She was beautiful, the spitting image of Ababa, and a stark reminder that even when life doesn't turn out like you want, even when that miracle doesn't happen, there is no time to give up. There is always another who needs your help…they need your faith, because there is always hope that this time might be different.

In 2 Corinthians 4:8–9 it says, "We are afflicted in every way, but not crushed; perplexed, but not driven to despair; persecuted, but not forsaken; struck down, but not destroyed." I still believe in miracles. I have to. Even in my disappointment, God is still loving and working, and He brings comfort and healing. Perhaps this is one of the greatest miracles of all. He is a good God, and it helps me to remember that when my heart is broken, His heart is broken too.

If your heart is wounded by disappointment, unanswered prayer, or miracles you have yet to see, fight the temptation to allow it to make your world grow smaller. If you don't, life may crush in all around you. Instead, try these things:

- Remember the wonder of God you have seen in the past.
- Focus on the good in your life now.
- Release any bitterness—forgive.
- Open your heart to the possibilities once again.

Let me encourage you with this: sometimes those things that most concern you, those things you are praying and asking God to stop, are the very things He will actually use to bring your miracle.

One day we got a call that instantly brought our world to a screeching halt. It was our daughter, the same one who lost her flip-flops many years before. She was seven months pregnant with our first grandchild when her water broke. Instantly, I was begging: "God no, it's too soon!"

It was a frightening road fraught with difficulties. Eventually Taylor was rushed into surgery for an emergency C-section. As our beautiful granddaughter was born, the doctor looked up and declared this was a miracle. In her hand she held the umbilical cord, which contained a huge blood clot, an umbilical thrombosis. She explained that if it weren't for the early birth and emergency C-section, we could have easily lost both the baby and our daughter. When we were praying, "God, no," He was already in the midst of His miracle and that thing we feared most, her water breaking early, was the tool He used to make it happen.

I believe in a big God. Uninhibited by any obstacle. Unfettered by impossibility. My world is large because my God is. God is a God of wonders—wonders I want to always be open to, to see and appreciate. Psalm 105:5 reminds us to, "Remember the wondrous works that he has done, his miracles, and the judgments he uttered." And Psalm 119:18 says, "Open my eyes, that I may behold wondrous things out of your law." Make your world large. Don't chase miracles but do chase God. Acknowledge how big He is. See the possibilities. Give your adventures room to breathe. Blow out the limits. Believe.

STEP BY STEP

- Consider the things that have made your world smaller and release them, such as:
  - o Busyness
  - o Disappointment
  - o Unbelief

- Make a list of the works of God in your life, the little winks and the big answers to prayer.

- Welcome belief back into your life. Open your heart to the wonder of unlimited possibilities and enlarge your world!

SECTION III

SPLASHING JOY

Joy does not simply happen to us.
We have to choose joy
and keep choosing it every day.
—Henri Nouwen—

CHAPTER 11

THE GRATEFULNESS AMPLIFICATION

*I would maintain that thanks are
the highest form of thought, and that gratitude
is happiness doubled by wonder.*
—G. K. Chesterton—

You are coming along! You're learning to chase after the wonder all around you and activate your adventure mentality, stoking its fires and keeping it alive and well, and hopefully you're stepping out in action and seeing an exciting shift in your life. You are developing your sense of wonder, taking the time to acknowledge the amazing things that stop you in your tracks as well as noticing the simple daily joys that continually bring smiles to your face. Now it's time to rev up that engine and kick this lifelong adventure up a notch. That's right, it gets even better from here. Don't settle yet, there is much more ahead. There is more to this chase.

There is a very important ingredient that, when added to this equation of a sense of wonder plus an adventure mentality, will exponentially multiply your results. Your adventures and your life get bigger and better when they are overflowing with joy. This joy, this secret sauce is the pièce de résistance propelling you to new levels. It's true, think about it! You can have great adventures and discover spectacular wonders along the way, but if you don't let them sink in—if you don't marinate in them and let them reduce down to a lasting joy, not just temporary happiness—it is all fleeting.

And here is one of the best parts: joy has the uncanny ability to fill our lives so full that there is enough to splash over onto anyone in our wake! That is my desire—for the joy God gives me to splash out into the unsuspecting lives of others around me (see Phil. 1:25–26). I love being sneaky like that!

If you want that too, there is a brilliant way to make your life a happy home for joy to reside. This powerful suggestion is a matter of the heart and one anyone can implement. Here it is—be grateful. Gratitude acts as a multiplier, a booster increasing the power of the wonder, amazement, and joy you experience, and it is key to a peaceful, meaningful, and fulfilling life.

I find G. K. Chesterton's quote absolutely perfect: "Gratitude is happiness doubled by wonder." Living in a state of gratitude, maintaining a thankful heart, is far more than just a pleasantry; it is a powerful amplifier that can move you from being happy when your circumstances are right to a joy that permeates your being.

Okay, curmudgeons, I can practically hear your eyes rolling. Stop scoffing, don't skim ahead, and please just give me a little bit of latitude. I understand your hesitance—life is not all puppies and butterflies, but isn't it worth a few more minutes to potentially uncover a slight adjustment that could increase your overall life satisfaction? Ask yourself: "What if this little adventurer is right? What if my heart could grow three sizes this day? What have I got to lose?"

Whoever you are, whatever you are thinking, I'm not going to allow you the excuse that this concept of gratitude just doesn't fit your personality. I promised friendly little pushes when you need them, and this is one of them. I understand some people are more prone to negativity while others are more naturally positive but that's not what I am talking about here. Gratitude isn't about pessimism or optimism; gratitude is all about training, so we are headed to boot camp. Get ready to learn how to seek out and nurture gratefulness and joy in your life.

Everyone loves the idea of joy. It may at times appear fleeting, but it is real, and God has it for you if you want it. Psalm 16:11 says it so beautifully: "In your presence there is fullness of joy; at your right hand are pleasures forevermore." The interesting thing about joy is it's all around us; the more you acknowledge it, the more you'll find. It's out there, one of the fabulous side effects of wonder; we just need to remain dedicated to the chase.

Consider this concept of chasing wonder and its accompanying joy. It takes just a little extra effort; joy may not just fall into your lap, but it does want to be caught. To be good hunters, we must develop our skills. Some actions and attitudes draw joy to us, and others chase it away.

Most days before work, I head out for an early morning walk. It's one of my favorite times of the day; it's not only good exercise but the time with God is priceless. I enjoy the crisp morning air, beautiful sunrises, and the sun sparkling through the mist of early morning sprinklers. I tell God the things that are on my mind, spend some time listening, and finish ready to start my day with a spring in my step. (An important note: I am *not* a morning person; this does not come easily to me. It has been a decision and a commitment, and one I am always glad I made.)

This also means I spend a lot of time in my tennis shoes. Not long ago I got a new pair that fit well and seemed perfect except for one thing—one very annoying thing. They had a squeak. A nerve-racking squeak with each and every step. Squeak. Squeak. Squeak.

For a while I was patient, hopeful that in time they would break in and stop their whining, but no such luck. They continued to nag at me mile after mile. Their unrelenting complaining kept grating on me and becoming seemingly louder and louder until I could hear little else. How could I listen for God's still, small voice over this roaring squeak? Before long the sunrises weren't as pretty, and the mist didn't sparkle as brilliantly, until one day I could take no more. The shoes went into the Salvation Army donation bin to bless someone else with their squawking.

How easy it is to be like those shoes—complaining incessantly until those around us can't tolerate it anymore. Or worse, they become like us. Complaining is highly contagious. I don't want to be a complainer. I don't want to be blinded to beauty by annoyances or miss the many things I have to be grateful for because I am solely focused on those things I am not. I want to be full of joy so it splashes out around me and not be tripped up in that pursuit by the minefield of complaints along the way.

Sure, we all complain sometimes. But nothing squeezes the life and the joy out of an adventure like complaining. It turns you into that annoying kid in the back seat, repeatedly asking, "Are we there yet?" all the while missing the incredible wonder out the window. Complaining is like releasing a giant boa constrictor and saying, "Go ahead, squeeze away! Squeeze the joy out because I'm not all that fond of having fun anyway."

I'll freely admit, I can be a person who is easily annoyed. When things don't go the way I think they should, when people don't act the way I think they should, even when God doesn't respond as I prefer He would (yes, how childish and presumptuous is that?), I have been known to get frustrated, roll my eyes, or do some good old-fashioned complaining to anyone who will listen. I've been working hard to change that. When I become that person, I realize I'm not as happy as I usually am. There is an air about that person I really don't like. The joy around me dissipates. And to top it all off, I'm even less cute when I look in the mirror.

I have learned to pay attention to my danger signs. For example, I am more easily annoyed and apt to complain when I'm tired or don't feel well. Sometimes small annoyances pile up, seem larger than they really are, and eventually threaten to overwhelm me like an avalanche. When I notice the signs, I need to respond accordingly. I commence with countermeasures by stirring up my gratitude.

"HEY, BIG GUY, SUN'S GETTING REAL LOW"

I won't be so shallow as to say just count your blessings one by one and all the ugly will go away. It is true in theory, but I believe you deserve more realism than that. It works differently for me. When I make the choice, the concerted effort, to exchange my bad attitude for one of overt thankfulness, the big green Hulk in me calms down. (Thus *The Avengers* reference above.) I purposefully focus on the things for which I am grateful—not so much making a list, but conscientiously looking for those things and acknowledging them when I encounter them. Before long, I notice my joy returning. I still may be unhappy with the current circumstances, but the reflection in the mirror looks much better again.

It has a lot to do with what you choose to carry. When we go for walks with our dog, Winston, like all good neighbors we take along poop bags. When he drops his little payload, we bag it up. We have learned a handy trick so we don't have to carry the stinky bag with us the entire time. We drop it at a corner and then pick it up when we come back by on the way home. The lesson here is simple: don't carry the poop in your life any longer than you have to—and then, always clean up after yourself.

You may feel like you are carrying a stinky little bag with you much of the time, holding on to the frustrations, annoyances, and hurts of life. If you do, you will begin to smell bad too, and the wonders you've been dedicated to chasing will hightail it and run in the opposite direction. Put it down. Then, at the right time, get rid of it. Let it go and clean up the mess it left behind. Perhaps you need to apologize to someone or correct a contagious negative attitude you shared. When you drop that bag, you can choose instead to focus on and be grateful for the beautiful day, the exercise you are getting, the time with your husband and puppy, or whatever applies in your situation and brings you joy.

There's an old song that says it really well:

Turn your eyes upon Jesus,
Look full in His wonderful face,
And the things of earth will grow strangely dim,
In the light of His glory and grace.

It is a matter of focus…a decision…and it works. Proverbs 17:22 says, "A joyful heart is good medicine, but a crushed spirit dries up the bones." A joyful heart is a grateful heart. It pays extra attention to life's daily pleasures and the unexpected blessings. It is a heart of adventure and it brings life to those it touches.

There are many things in life for which to be grateful: health, love, beauty... These are the easy targets. The real challenge is to dig deeper and look for gratitude even in the midst of the hard stuff:

- A friend who stays by your side when others don't
- An accident that wasn't as bad as it could have been
- A good memory in a time of grief
- One part of your body that works when another doesn't

I encourage you to work on a list of your own. It may not be easy, but I promise you, it will change you.

I told you there are times when I have an upcoming trip, but I just don't feel like going. I don't really want to pack and unpack, do loads of laundry, eat food I may not like, and endure the potential jet lag. There is little worse than heading out on a long journey cranky and complaining. Adventure mentality officially squelched! So rather than focusing on what I *don't* want to do, I make a conscious turn to focus on the fact that *I get to go*. Not *have to*—I *get to*! I get to do this amazing thing so few people ever experience. I get to see new things and meet new people. I get to live a new adventure. I nurture the gratitude in my heart and inevitably, I'm ready and grateful when the time comes to head out the door.

I WILL NEVER FORGET YOU

In 2015, an 8.1 magnitude earthquake devastated a vast area of Nepal, killing nearly nine thousand people and leaving 3.5 million homeless. Hand of Hope began helping immediately, providing desperately needed supplies and helping to rebuild. Our team traveled to Nepal, to a particularly remote village along the edge of the Himalayas. When we arrived, we found the dirt road to the village was washed out by monsoon rains, and the only way in and out was to hike up and down the mountainside. So we left the vehicle, carried our equipment, and began walking.

It was a long, hot day of trudging up and down the mountainside, shooting for television in the intense Nepali heat and humidity. Afternoon thunderstorms only served to intensify the experience. At the end of the day I was exhausted. I stood in the shade of a tree looking up at the long uphill path we had yet to hike to get back to the main road and felt a few complaints working their way up.

That is when a small band of four little girls approached, determined to take me on a tour of their village. I had no intention of joining them. They grabbed my arms, two on each side, and it soon became obvious that the choice wasn't mine. They began pulling me uphill while they giggled and chattered. In broken English they told me all about their lives and their experiences when the recent earthquake struck. As they dragged me up and down the dirt paths through the destroyed homes, I quickly realized that tired or not, these are the moments that matter most. Divine appointments that God gives us—this is where the true wonder lies. My original annoyance turned to gratitude and then to delight, ushering in an afternoon I will always cherish.

I told them how impressed I was with their English and they laughed as I attempted to pronounce their names. We darted from place to place as they shared story after story. Where did they get this energy? Mine was spent but I found it renewed by the joy of these sweet girls. Joy splashes over. Along the way they flitted around like fireflies and picked bouquets of wildflowers for me. Frankly, the flowers were hot and scratchy in my sweaty hands, but I wouldn't put them down for anything. They were precious gifts.

They told me about the earthquake. One called it, "The most afraid I have ever been. I thought we would all die." They still wouldn't sleep inside in fear of another quake and the building falling down on them. I asked how their families and homes were. Their families survived with some broken bones. They told me about friends who'd lost parents and others with crushed arms or legs. As for their houses, they clapped their hands together— "Flat," they said. "Come, we'll show you," and off we went, running again.

They told me everyone in the village had been very sad since the earthquake and how our visit made them happy again. "It's very kind of you to visit from so far away," they said. They were quick to point out that they knew I had come from far away because my skin was "very light and funny," and we all laughed hard. "But beautiful," they said. I told them they were all very beautiful and I introduced them to the "selfie."

They wanted to sing me a song and though I couldn't understand a word, the tune was sweet. Then they asked me to teach them one, so I began singing "Jesus Loves Me." They repeated each line after me and soon we were singing together. "That is a very nice song," they said. Then one sweet little girl asked me if I believed in Jesus. I told them all about Him, how He is alive and with us right now and how He does love them very much. She said her parents don't believe that, but since He was my friend, He would be hers too.

My heart melted. They asked to sing the song again and again, and we sang together until I begged for mercy. "I can't sing anymore; I'm out of breath."

After a tour of every square inch of the village, we finally reached the top of the mountainside where we had parked our vehicles. There, in a slightly more populated area, one of the girls showed me her mother's small store, which had survived the earthquake—a miracle in itself. She proudly introduced me as her new friend, and then I went on to our van. Just before we drove away, she ran back to me one final time to give me another gift, a piece of candy from the store. One last hug and off she went, calling, "I won't forget you!" as she waved goodbye.

I think of those girls often. I'm grateful I got to be there with them. I'm still amazed God connected me with those four small girls halfway around the world on a steep hillside that few people will ever visit. I'm thankful for the wonder I found there in the aftermath of a terrible natural disaster. I am grateful we could help in their time of need. I am thankful for the precious gifts of flowers and a tiny piece of wrapped candy. How wonderful that I got to tell a tiny band of sweet girls, "Yes, Jesus loves you."

I believe God took my humble offering of gratitude, even when I felt like grumbling, and used it to change the memory of a long, exhausting day into one of pure joy. And I pray He did something eternal in their hearts as well. I find when I live generously and seek out new ways to give and to help people, extraordinary adventures pop up unexpectedly, everywhere.

When you are grateful, say so. Acknowledge it; say "Thank you," out loud. It's not about *feeling* gratitude—remember, gratitude is a choice. It isn't enough to think it. Unspoken gratitude is gratitude with its hands tied. It is half as effective. Activate that amplifier in your life, increase your joy and that of others. Tell the people you appreciate, thank you. Tell God, thank You. Let your gratitude drown out your complaining.

Your mission in this gratefulness boot camp is to capture the opportunities, not allowing one to slip through your fingers. Actively chase wonder and don't let it escape your notice or your thankfulness. That is when you will have more than enough joy for yourself and it will spill out all over the people around you.

STEP BY STEP

- Make the choice to live in gratitude. The excuse that your personality just isn't naturally overtly thankful is officially kicked to the curb.

- Stop yourself in your tracks when you begin to complain.

- Put down any little "poop bags" you are carrying right now. Apologize when and where you need to and clean up the mess before it becomes worse.

- Make a list of the more difficult-to-see things you are grateful for—the good even in the midst of the challenging.

- Say "Thank you!" as many times as you can, to as many people as you can. Say it out loud even if no one is there to hear it but God.

- Marinate in the joy you find, allowing it to seep deep into your being and fill up until it can't help but overflow and splash wonderfully all over the people around you.

CHAPTER 12

WALKING IN THEIR SHOES

If you walk the footsteps of a stranger,
you'll learn things you never knew
you never knew.
—Pocahontas—

Visualize yourself in a chase scene in your own action movie. You're in a fast car, like a Lamborghini or a Bugatti (after all, this is your imaginary movie so you should drive something fabulous). You're speeding through the streets, zipping in and out of tiny alleyways, and brushing off of parked cars. Just as you are about to catch up to your target, a large truck pulls out in front of you and you are brought to a screeching halt. This is how it sometimes feels when you are chasing wonder and joy. Just when you are almost there, something unexpected and frustrating pops up, completely derailing your progress and sucking the fun out of your entire adventure.

When you are actively pursuing something—*anything*—you need a solid strategy to catch it. We are committed to this chase, so let's continue to talk strategy. I can tell you where joy is—finding it is the easy part. Galatians 5:22 tells us that joy is a fruit of God's Spirit. That means when you invite Jesus into your life, joy comes as a part of the deal. You have it. But I picture it like a bottle of Italian dressing. Inside that bottle are all the seasonings, or for this purpose, the fruit of the Spirit—love, joy, peace, patience, kindness, goodness, faithfulness, gentleness, and self-control—all settled at the bottom. They are there, but you need to shake them up to access them.

God wants to fill our lives with joy, but the weight of the world and the stress of life can push that joy down. That gratitude we just explored acts like a lightning rod for joy. We can clear the way for it to flow freely by using gratitude to shake up that bottle. Don't allow all the good stuff to settle; keep it stirred up with a thankful heart. You see, joy isn't just an option; throughout the Bible God commands us to rejoice. In fact, it's one of the most repeated directives in the Bible.

Here are just a few examples:

- Be glad in the Lord and rejoice, you righteous; And shout for joy, all *you* upright in heart (Psalm 32:11 NKJV)!

- You shall rejoice in the LORD, *And* glory in the Holy One of Israel (Isa 41:16 NKJV).
- Rejoice in the LORD always. Again I will say, rejoice! (Phil. 4:4 NKJV).

God tells us to celebrate, circulating that joy throughout our life and overflowing to others.

Be aware, God is not fooled by empty words. You have much to be thankful for, but you may not always realize it. An excellent strategy to activate sincere gratitude is to interrupt our love affair with ourselves and take the time to walk in someone else's shoes. I know you have your own issues; I do too. But given the opportunity to recognize it, there is always something to be grateful for and someone with greater needs than our own.

I was profoundly struck by this truth last year in Ethiopia when I met a very young mother named Mekides in extraordinary circumstances. As we were talking, I asked her a question I often ask mothers: "What are your dreams for your baby daughter?" Her answer blew me away.

Mekides had escaped the red-light district in Addis Ababa, one of the most horrific places you can imagine. The streets are lined with door after door leading to tiny dark rooms only slightly larger than the beds that occupy them. Strings of a few colored lights beckon men into the rooms to use and abuse empty, hopeless women. Their blank stares silently scream out their pain. Perhaps most shocking is the children who wander these streets alone at night or wait outside the rooms as their mothers usher in man after man. Infants are literally stashed away in boxes under the beds.

Being in the red-light district never fails to sicken me. Places like this should not exist, but they do. Mekides was once hopelessly trapped in that dreadful place, and her infant daughter, Devora, slept in a box under her bed. But not anymore. She escaped to a rescue home where she was safe, respected, and prepared for a career she can be proud of, ensuring they never have to go back there. They were also showered with the love of God.

Mekides told me how her own dream had now come true; she has a new career as a hairstylist. But it was her next words that completely caught me off guard. I asked her about her dreams for her daughter and she answered, "I want her to be like you." Hot tears instantly sprang to my eyes. She wanted her daughter to be like me. I was so very humbled because I knew it wasn't about me personally, but about the blessings I too often take for granted. She went on to explain, "Like you, a fulfilled girl, a fulfilled woman—she will become successful and helping other women."

The magnitude of her words hit me like a sledgehammer, and I was overwhelmed with gratitude and a sense of responsibility. I am exceptionally blessed to live a life where I am fulfilled, where I know the goodness of God, and am able to help others. A life where I experience God's wonder on a regular basis. When I get dissatisfied with life's circumstances, and I do at times, I remember Mekides's words and I choose gratitude. I simply can't thank God enough.

It is difficult to put yourself in someone else's shoes, but nothing opens your eyes to gratitude in quite the same way. This young woman's freedom and dignity were stripped from her in the vilest of ways; she was a mother who desperately loved her daughter and wanted the world for her. As a woman and mother, I couldn't fathom that kind of pain. Such things are difficult to even consider, to put myself in her place or to think of my daughters suffering in such a way, and yet I must, or I'm not doing her justice. If she can survive these terrible things, I can at least attempt to understand them. And out of that deep consideration grows empathy, determination, and magnified gratitude.

MANY SHOES TO WALK IN

I have had many opportunities to walk in other people's shoes and each time, I grow and am better for it. At the height of the AIDS epidemic, I spent five years documenting the experience of Clinton Engel, a gay man with AIDS. What started as an arrangement between a television producer and a stranger grew into a loving friendship as he shared most every aspect of his physical, emotional, and spiritual journey. Through him, I learned about the frustration and betrayal of a physical body growing weaker and weaker. I got a glimpse into the pain of societal rejection. I experienced God's hand at work from a very different perspective.

In the end, I grieved the loss of my friend and was grateful for having known him. My life and my heart for people are different today because he allowed me to walk in his shoes.

I once walked with a woman and her three children to fetch water through the jungle in Peru. They described how they would encounter dangerous wildlife, venomous snakes, and strangers, which can be the most threatening of all. When we reached the water, it was dark and dirty. They drink from the same source that animals bathe and defecate in. We collected the water in buckets and pans and began the journey back. Water is heavy; a gallon of water weighs about eight pounds, so imagine carrying a five-gallon bucket for miles. Even a smaller container is a lot of weight to balance on a small child's head. I tried it and was not successful, which added some levity to our trek.

That simple experience changed me. Ever since, when I turn on a faucet flowing with clean water, I am exceptionally grateful because I understand the alternative. I haven't lived exactly what they have, but I have taken a walk in their shoes.

There are hundreds of thousands of homeless children around the world, and one evening, late at night, I shocked a family of six brothers and sisters by stopping to spend time with them. You see, they are more likely to be threatened by people than to be approached with kindness. Each day is a struggle for survival for these kids, and it is evident by the deep sorrow in their eyes.

I sat down with those kids, right there on the street, and they shared their world with me. They showed me how they find a spot to sleep each night, laying cardboard down for a bed and draping filthy plastic over the top like a tent to protect them from the weather. They told me about the dangers they face each night. They take turns sleeping so they can watch each other's back. When we said goodbye there was an obvious expression of "thank you" even though the words were never said—an unspoken gratitude for taking the time to listen, for showing sincere interest in them in a world where most people consider them trash to be swept away.

In every one of these experiences, I was the person who was most impacted. Walking in their shoes, opening up my heart to them, and taking the time to be a part of their lives, acted like a turbo booster for my level of gratitude, increasing the joy in my life to a place I didn't even realize was possible. I don't know whose shoes you may walk in down the road, but when the opportunity arises, take it. It will teach you so much, it will jettison your gratitude, and you will never be the same.

THE BEAUTIFUL FACES OF ADVENTURE

I said this before, and I mean it with all my heart—as we aspire to chasing wonder, we will find it most in the people along the way. *The people we meet are our greatest adventures.* Sometimes when I least expect it, my mind wanders far from the comfort and safety of my home to these faraway places. My thoughts hover in tiny grass huts and shelters made of scrap metal and plastic; in abandoned inner-city buildings where children take shelter; and in trash dumps no one should call home, yet thousands do. I'm thinking of friends who don't enjoy the basic necessities of life that I can easily take for granted, like a good meal and a safe place to lay my head. I don't take those things for granted anymore.

I vividly see their faces. Most are not what you would call classically beautiful by the world's standards, but without doubt, they are some of the loveliest faces you'll ever find. Big smiles full of rotten teeth set in leathery, wrinkled skin; evidence of a hard life in the sun. Some eyes twinkle with joy even in the most difficult circumstances, while others radiate a tangible sorrow that pierces the soul. There's no looking away; young and old they are captivating. These are absolutely some of the most beautiful people in the world.

Perhaps our current standard of beauty—the next-top-model theory—misses the mark. There may be something more beautiful than a flawless face and perfect proportions. Instead, the key may be to see people through God's eyes. In 1 Peter 3:4 it says it is "the hidden person of the heart, with the incorruptible *beauty* of a gentle and quiet spirit, which is very precious in the sight of God." When their clothes are dirty and torn, He sees royalty. Those crooked grins bring a smile to His face. How His eyes light up when they look to Him!

God's overwhelming love for us is the thing that should stir up the most gratitude within us. *That* is what fills me with joy. It's when we take our mind off ourselves and consider the rest of the world that God's heart is beating in our chest. And you don't have to travel to another country or experience the worst of humanity to walk in someone else's shoes. Everyone craves to be understood. Everyone has something to teach us.

Think again about that chase scene from the movie of your life. Rather than recklessly driving through the streets, chasing a mysterious target and never quite succeeding, now see yourself walking peacefully down the sidewalk, smiling and talking to friends, and getting to know new people. With each interaction, you are discovering that elusive thing you were chasing in futility and seizing more joy, taking in greater wonder.

Talk to the widow in your neighborhood. Help the single mother in your church. Get to know your boss—she may need a friend. Do it for them, but also, do it for you. Your own adventures will evolve into much more than meaningless activity, boredom will be squeezed from the equation, a sense of fulfilling and gratifying purpose will bloom, and that joy will flow from your changed life.

STEP BY STEP

- Choose someone.
- Make a plan to get to know them in a deeper way, to walk in their shoes.
- Shake up your gratitude and let the joy splash over.
- Repeat.

CHAPTER 13

COMPLETE ACCEPTANCE

You wouldn't worry so much about what others think
of you if you realized how seldom they do.
—Eleanor Roosevelt—

Something lovely happens when someone notices us, when we receive a compliment, when we receive enough "likes" on social media. It feels good, releases happy endorphins, tells us we are loved, gives us value, validates our existence—whoa there! I'm going too far with this; it's absurdly overstated. But doesn't it feel that way at times? If only someone would encourage me…if they would notice what I've done for them, how hard I'm working, then I would be happy. So, what happens to your joy when you don't receive that approval?

Recently our dog, Sir Winston Churchill (you can call him

Winston, he's not big on formality), who is a cute shaggy little fella, got a bit matted and had to be shaved. I am hanging my head in shame as I write this because it was, of course, our fault. We try to keep him nicely combed out, but his hair is quite thick and coarse, something like a tiny sheep, and the truth is, we failed. When we picked him up from the groomer it was shocking. He was shaved to the skin. He was so tiny, like a naked mole rat with a fluffy tail and long ears.

But that's not the worst of it. Winston was visibly embarrassed. At first, he wouldn't even look at us. He didn't want to go outside and I'm fairly certain he did not want the neighborhood dogs to look upon his shame. It was as if he knew that the other dogs would whisper behind his back, or worse, howl it throughout the streets—"Winston looks ridiculous." Now, if dogs can get embarrassed and want approval—dogs who are unashamed to explore one another's hind ends—it is a given that people desire approval even more.

Of course, we all enjoy compliments, I certainly do. I like approval and validation as much as anyone else, and to prove it, I'll admit I was also embarrassed to walk our freshly shaved pup around the neighborhood. All those comments of "Oh my, what happened to him?" got really old after a few blocks.

How important to you is the validation of others? Do you need it to feel significant? Do you pursue great adventures so that you can tell people and they will be impressed? Earlier I said I believe in having stories to share, but are you telling those stories to make yourself feel more important, or to connect with someone else in a way that enriches both of your lives?

If your goal is to impress others and to gain their approval, I can guarantee you'll be disappointed. People will never be able to give you what you really need, and living to please them is a prolonged, painful journey to nowhere. A real joy sucker. You'll never compile enough compliments or accolades to fill that tank, and instead of being satisfied, you'll always be scrapping for more. As I said, we all like approval, but we can't base our life choices on or determine our personal worth from it.

I had a "friend" (please notice the quotes around the word "friend") who nearly always followed a compliment with a little jab. She would say things like, "You are so cute, and if you did something with that hair, you could be really pretty." Or, "You did a good job. It could have been better, but it was good." And then there's, "I like that outfit, but those shoes!" It's a good thing I'm basically a secure person or my interactions with her could have left me feeling pretty bad about myself.

After enough of this, I didn't choose to spend a lot of time with her. I realized no matter what I did I was never going to gain her approval and I could see she didn't really respect our relationship. The point is, don't seek after someone's approval so much that you are willing to put up with a bad relationship to get it. Most of us have a little bit of high school still in us. We want to be one of the cool crowd and be popular, thinking, perhaps, "If the right person notices me, I'll finally feel good about myself." That attitude is a good way to chase the wonder right out of your life and to move into a very unhappy place.

HANGING WITH THE COOL KIDS

Throughout my career, I have had the pleasure of interviewing and spending time with several well-known people, including celebrities, musical artists, politicians, and professional athletes—people who many would consider important and might even attempt to impress. Some of these people were a real pleasure to be with; time with others was unremarkable; and a couple were downright rude. In other words, they were just like everyone else. A special few had the ability to make me feel like I was the most important person in the world at that moment, while others left me feeling invisible or, worse, like an inconvenience.

Lessons learned from interactions with the rich and famous:

- They are much like everyone else and their approval is no more or less important.
- Charlton Heston did indeed have the voice of God; I still hear his voice when I read the Bible.
- I desperately want to be one of those people who make everyone feel valued and important.
- I can now spin a basketball on the end of my finger, thanks to Harlem Globetrotter Meadowlark Lemon.

I love meeting people, well-known or not, and appreciate benefiting from their experience and talent, but I shouldn't be more interested in those with more notoriety or influence. No matter how important they are, they cannot make me more important, so rather than trying to gain something from them, my goal should be to offer them something they may need—a warm smile, a good laugh, time with someone who treats them like any normal friend.

I'm honored to have friends all over the world who enrich my life, but perhaps none more than those who have nothing to offer me. No influence, no power or promotion, no riches. And for me, children top the list. In my mind there is a cherished album of kids around the world who have stolen my heart. My Elsie, Blessy, Roja, Phillip, Pepe, Isayas, Priscilla…the list goes on and on. Their love flows freely and is not based on my status or appearance, what I can do for them, or who I know. The joy that these children have brought to my life can't be overestimated.

I know a particularly wonderful group of preschoolers who showed me the power of unconditional acceptance and love. They are some of the happiest children I have encountered anywhere in the world, in spite of the abject poverty that surrounds them. They are led by an amazing teacher, Miss Erica, who has devoted her life to teaching, protecting, loving, and sharing Jesus with them. They taught me that joy doesn't depend on our circumstances and can be found anywhere.

Arriving at Miss Erica's tiny school in Namibia, we were greeted with laughter, songs, and hugs. We were instantly family.

At the end of our first day together, we parted with a huge group hug from dozens of children, the kind that pulls you to the ground in sheer delight. When we returned the next morning, the children ran toward me and said, "Oh, Ginger, we have missed you so much!" like I had been gone for months. My heart was goo in their hands, and I knew there was no better expression of love and gratitude that I could ever ask for. I found so much wonder in their midst. I don't need popularity, public accolades, or the acceptance of everyone I meet when my heart is full of this kind of no-strings-attached love, which I could never earn but is freely given.

ON A SHELF

Another way we strive for value and worth is in success and professional recognition. These are good things, and you should be pleased when hard work pays off, but again, these alone will never give you the complete fulfillment that you need.

I had accumulated five Emmy nominations before I finally heard my name called. Five. Talk about always the bridesmaid. It felt great for my work to be acknowledged by my peers. Mine is a regional Emmy, which means it's not quite as large as those other ones, but the smile it brought to my face was just as big. After years of working in television, I was happy to be holding the little guy. It was a good moment.

A few years later, in a tiny village in the African bush, we had been working hard all day sharing heartbreaking stories of need such as I had never seen before. As the sun set, a group of tribal leaders was meeting in a circle around a fire outside. Through an interpreter they invited me over and asked me to join them. To my surprise they presented me with a gift, a lovely clay honey pot decorated with tiny, white shells. They explained that their hearts were touched by the words I shared with our television audience regarding kindness and God's love for all people, and they offered me this simple yet beautiful gift to show their gratitude. I was deeply touched.

When we arrived back in the city, I was approached by several people in the hotel lobby who noticed the honey pot. They explained to me that this was a great honor in their culture. Gaining a deeper understanding into the significance of this special gift brought even more tears to my eyes.

The clay pot sits on a shelf at home close to the Emmy and other professional awards—completely overshadowing them. No one who sees it knows what it represents, but it means a great deal to me. Hearing my name called and receiving that Emmy was an achievement I thought would change my life, but it didn't compare to the joy I received sitting around that fire in a place no one would ever see.

Throughout our home you also will find many other important things. A tiny scrap of paper saying, "You are so 'speshal' to me Mommy." Candid snapshots reminding us of wonderful memories, like the silly faces our family can't help but make together everywhere we go. These photos and notes of love and gratitude represent the moments I cherish most of all…too many to count and more precious than any accomplishment or award.

The world sees a public honor such as an Emmy, Oscar, Grammy, or [enter your appropriate award here] as a life-defining accomplishment, providing acceptance and validation. But these things do not define a life. It is actually the quiet moments that tend to sneak by unnoticed that are most significant. These are the things that bring us the deepest joy. These are the things we find as we chase wonder.

Acknowledgements are important, but more than objects that can sit on a shelf or fill a house, it is the things of the heart that define a life as successful. Relationships with friends and family, memories and adventures enjoyed together, kindness to strangers, and above all a relationship with Jesus. You can't put any of them on display, but they fill the heart much more completely.

We are all looking for something. We seek it in encouraging words, in the acceptance of people, accomplishment, and success. You may have always wanted to be noticed by that particular group or a special someone. You may have spent most of your life longing for the approval of a parent you may never receive. You and I can choose to spin our wheels trying to please everyone with whom we come in contact or we can take a different path—one that is much more satisfying.

CHICK FLICKS

I'm not a very girly girl, but I must admit I have a soft spot for sappy love stories. There is something about a tale of pure, undeniable love that draws me. You know the story. Boy meets girl. Boy pursues girl. The craziness of life threatens to come between them until that breathtaking moment when the two are finally brought together (usually in a rainstorm) and an audible "aww" slips out of the crowd. In the end, girl and boy live happily ever after in perfect bliss.

Wow, that *was* sappy. But admit it, you feel the same. It's universal—in every culture, women and men alike enjoy stories of the kind of love that changes a person forever.

Books and movies like *Pride and Prejudice*, *The Notebook*, *Sweet Home Alabama*, and *Gladiator* make us feel all warm and squishy inside. (Yes, I said *Gladiator*, because I believe it is a love story at its heart, and I need a little adventure to counteract all of that sugar.) But there is one love story that endures like none other and changes the life of anyone who will allow it—*the story of Christ's love for us*. It has all the necessary elements of the perfect love story: passion, tragedy, redemption, and a happy ending. But this story is better because it's absolutely true, and this time, *you* are the lucky girl (or guy, of course). You are the object of affection, and when the curtain closes, this perfect and unconditional love is yours forever.

This love story is the answer to everything we have been discussing in this chapter. It's the reason you can quit worrying about everyone else's acceptance, because you have complete validation that overshadows them all. This is your answer, a revelation that will set you free and fill you with a joy that never runs out. It is the greatest wonder of all.

I'm not talking about the mechanics of becoming a Christian; I'm asking you to finally welcome and bask in the fullness of God's love for you. This releases you from the constant struggle to win people's approval; it just isn't necessary because it doesn't compare. You don't have to work to impress them anymore to feel important. You are so important that the Creator of the universe gave everything for you. You are whole and loved completely.

You've got to love that scene in the movie *Jerry Maguire* where Tom Cruise comes bursting into a room of disgruntled women complaining about their sad love lives and tells Renée Zellweger he loves her and wants her back. He says, "You complete me." She answers with the famous line, "You had me at hello." (Sniff, sniff.)

Like Jerry said, "we live in a cynical world," a world where acceptance and unconditional love are difficult to come by. But you can have it, right now, if you want it. It won't come from Tom Cruise or any romantic relationship. It won't come through position, success, accomplishment, or accolades. It won't even come from your friends or family. Don't go chasing accolades or approval thinking you'll find real wonder. There is very little that is real in what you find there. God's love is the one treasure that will truly complete you, and in it you will find the most joy and the greatest adventure of your life!

STEP BY STEP

- Take an inventory of how much you seek the approval and acknowledgment of others. Be honest with yourself.
- Is there someone whose approval you have always sought and never received? A parent, sibling, boss, or spouse, perhaps? Realize you are just as valuable without their approval and let it go once and for all.
- Really consider the incredible love God has for you. Don't disregard it or argue with Him; His love for you is a fact. Whether it's a refreshing reminder or perhaps the first time you've ever chosen to believe, allow it to soak into your heart and fill you to completion.
- Allow the awareness of God's perfect love to replace your need to please others.
- Now go watch your favorite chick flick.

CHAPTER 14

THE GENEROSITY PRINCIPLE

We make a living by what we get,
but we make a life by what we give.
—Winston Churchill—

I could see him skipping through the field toward us. It was not a pretty area; the village was very poor and some people might see only the poverty, but somehow in this moment, the scene was lovely. A young boy running carefree through a field of tall grass. He was laughing and waving, carrying something in his hand. As he got closer, I could see what it was—a *huge* mushroom, probably eight inches across the top. He was obviously very proud as he came running after me to present this gift. He wore a smile across his face that absolutely dwarfed the mushroom.

We were visiting this small village in India where we are honored to provide food, basic education, and a whole lot of love to kids who have little else. Most of these children depended on us for their only good meal of the day. And the attention they receive and love of Jesus they soak up changes their world like nothing else could.

Spending time with and getting to know children in places like this all over the world is one of my greatest joys, and in spite of the terrible circumstances they endure, their unstoppable joy always splashes over onto me.

His name was Philip and he was nine years old. We spent some time together, played some games in the courtyard, and then it was time to go. There is never enough time. As our team was packing up and walking back to our vehicle, I heard a voice and turned to see what it was. In the distance I saw Philip and instantly knew I would never forget the sight of him running across that field, waving something at me and calling my name. When he reached us, he proudly held out his precious gift, a mushroom so large it covered his entire hand as he held it by the long stem. I accepted it like it was gold, told him thank you, and gave him a big hug.

True generosity is a great wonder. It's not about monetary value, it is a matter of the heart. This was not just a gift, it was a loving sacrifice, extremely generous and very much appreciated. I held on to that mushroom for the rest of the evening. And Philip's gift brought both of us overwhelming joy.

I have been blessed by gifts like this from children in many countries, each one precious to me. I've cherished drawings, flowers, crafts, and big hugs from these who have so little of earthly value but still so very much to give. And I have learned some exceptionally valuable lessons, such as live generously and your joy will increase even more than the joy of those to whom you give. It is a principle of how God's wonder works.

Luke 6:38 says, "Give, and it will be given to you. A good measure, pressed down, shaken together, and running over will be poured into your lap" (NIV). Running over and splashing on everyone around you!

Don't fall into the wrong thinking that you have nothing to give. This generosity I am talking about is much broader than your finances, although that is one part of it. Living generously includes all you have to give to others. You can be generous with your:

- Kindness
- Time
- Comfort
- Wisdom
- Talent

The list is endless. You have what people need, and when you generously offer it, your joy increases, as does theirs.

Oh, there go those eyes rolling again. It is true we all are constantly asked to be generous. There are many needs in our world, and therefore, many requests. It's even possible you have seen me on your television making such a request, but I'm honored to ask because I know firsthand the joy it brings to all involved. I believe in the power of generosity. I have based my life on it.

So, here's a great question: Have you ever been disappointed when you were generous? What could an increase, or if you want a real adventure, a lifestyle of generosity possibly bring to your life?

A SIMPLE MEAL

I will never forget one particular meal and the family I shared it with. We met in a refugee camp in Greece. The Albadawy family fled their Syrian home with nothing more than the clothes on their backs. This father, mother, and two daughters were forced to leave behind their country, careers, and everything they owned to save their lives. In that camp, when they kindly invited me into their tent to share a meal, I knew they were offering no small gift. At first, I refused, not wanting to take any of the resources they so desperately needed, but they continued to insist, and I could see how important it was to them. All people desire and deserve dignity, and even in the direst of situations they want the opportunity to be generous themselves.

We sat together on folding cots and pillows on the floor of their tent and they passed one tiny can of something I couldn't identify and one plastic fork. As each person took a single bite and passed it along, I was overwhelmed with the full weight of their sacrifice of hospitality. This was the only food they had, and they were carefully rationing it to make it last, yet they selflessly and generously shared it with me, a stranger until just a few hours ago.

That day, the Albadawys taught me the true meaning of generosity. I thanked them profusely, and we parted with many hugs. They knew that in the midst of this terrible crisis, they were not forgotten. And I learned that generosity rarely goes only one way; it is a symbiotic relationship.

God gave His only son. That is what His gospel is all about, and when we generously share that kind of love, that is when our joy becomes so full it overflows onto others around us.

Living generosity opens the doors to so many incredible adventures and keeps us from other nasty things like selfishness and greed. When our focus is on living generously, we are actively looking for opportunities to share and to give. You can wake up every day with the intention of offering something of value to someone else, even if it's as simple as a smile. When we do that, we don't have time for selfishness, let alone boredom, because we are spending our time and energy in much more positive ways.

Generosity also helps us to maintain balance. Many things can easily morph from simple appreciation into greed or even addiction. Through generosity, we stay in balance by constantly considering what we have to offer. The best way to keep your life generous is to keep it simple enough that you are willing to let go—to keep it uncluttered from needless distraction. We constantly reassess what is important, releasing what isn't, and sharing what is.

Beware of barriers to generosity that will snatch away the progress we make in this area. Things such as:

- Envy
- Offense
- Wrong motives

Don't be the bitter person who sits back, complaining enviously about the exciting life your friend, neighbor, or coworker is living. Instead, go out there and make your own adventure by pushing aside that envy and gathering some joy of your own. Eventually, you could be so full of joy, you are even happy for them. That is what generosity does.

If you are holding on to offense in your heart, there may not be room for generosity. Offense says you are owed something, while generosity says you have something to offer. Offense says you want to get even, but generosity says you want to give freely. We have to choose one or the other. I've seen the bitterness offense cultivates and the wonder generosity attracts. I'm chasing wonder and joy that splashes over, so I'll choose generosity. I hope you will too. You can begin by letting go of the offense you're holding so you have a free hand to help someone else and grab some joy of your own.

HYENAS AT THE DOOR

Motives are everything. If you are generous for the wrong reasons, you really aren't generous at all. If your generosity is based on some sort of physical return on your investment, it won't accomplish much, and it won't last long.

Hyenas are known as the scavengers of the wild. One time our team was camping in tents deep in the African bush. At night, we could hear hyenas in the distance. They make an unusual sort of barking howl that really does resemble a bizarre laugh. Late one night I could hear heavy breathing and scratching at the tent wall. The hyenas came sneaking into the camp to scavenge whatever they could find. They are also dangerous, so men from the tribe who we were working with, the Datooga, stood guard with bows and arrows, which they were very good at using and ran them off. Even so, there was no wandering around outside alone late at night; no late-night potty runs. You just held it. Hyenas are not to be trusted.

Another time in Africa we were staying in grass huts and I could hear all kinds of ruckus outside including the sound of hooves and snorting. We were in Kenya, and Maasai men with their long red wraps and tall spears were watching over the area. They were on the lookout for lions, but what I heard outside was a friendly herd of zebras, so all was well. Motives are everything— you don't want hyenas or lions hanging around the camp, but a friendly group of zebras (which I learned is called a "dazzle") peacefully grazing is fine, and actually quite extraordinary.

Motives matter and God sees them even if no one else is sure. Don't be a hyena, laughing and acting like a friend only to scavenge what you can get in return. If you're going to be a lion, at least own it like one. But if you want a life of real significance, live with a pure generosity and let simple joy be your motive. It is the best return on investment you will ever find! So jump into this adventure of giving. Declutter your life of all the extraneous stuff that can get in the way and live generously. Open your big heart, flash some big smiles, and share some big love. You will love the wonder you discover!

STEP BY STEP

- What do you have to offer? Take an inventory and then look for opportunities to be generous with your assets.
- Consider your barriers to generosity and deal with them:
  - o Envy
  - o Offense
  - o Wrong motives
- Today, create an opportunity, choose someone, and be generous; then watch the wonder and joy grow, in both them and in you.

CHAPTER 15

A NIGHT WITH THE BUGS

If you cannot swallow your pride,
you are not thirsty enough for love.
—Pierre Jeanty—

I was thrilled when I walked down the pathway to the grass hut that would be my home for the next few days. It was amazing, exactly the kind of adventure I adore. The hut was right on the Zambezi River with a wooden deck looking down into the water and a fence keeping the crocodiles out. It was perfect.

Our team was in an extremely remote part of Zambia, documenting many outreach projects, including freshwater wells, feeding programs for children, and education for girls. Children gathering water from the river were being taken by crocodiles. Can you even imagine? Others died from drinking diseased water. Girls were being sold into marriage as soon as they reached puberty. It was an honor not only to be there but to have the opportunity to help make a real difference for these lovely, grateful people.

For me, sleeping in this grass hut was the icing on the cake. Or so I thought. Through the years I have come face-to-face with a lot of creepy crawly things, including insects, spiders, snakes, and critters of all types, usually with barely a flinch. I have more or less prided myself on the fact that I'm not afraid to get out there, get my hands dirty, do whatever is necessary, and endure those little nuisances that typically creep people out, and do it without complaining. I never wanted to be the girl on the trip who couldn't handle bugs, so I was pretty pleased with the fact that I was cool where they were concerned. Until that hut on the Zambezi.

The very first night revealed I was sharing my accommodations with an army of creepy creatures. When the sun went down, they came out, and in a big way. Some had six legs, some had eight, others had wings, and one of my roommates even had more than eight legs—*way* more. The carnage began with me killing a spider or two, but soon I couldn't help but notice they just kept coming and they appeared to be getting larger and larger. Then I discovered that the biggest wasps on the planet lived in the thatch roof and were accompanied by a large contingency of bees. I did have a mosquito net…which they loved. They would crawl all over it while I attempted to sleep. And next came the millipede, at least six inches long and the circumference of my index finger. This was the stuff of nightmares.

I had just about reached my limit when I moved a bed pillow to reveal the largest spider I have ever seen in the wild. I've seen some big spiders, including more than my share of tarantulas, but this monster dwarfed them all. Its legs stretched out to the size of my hand. I jumped and it scurried, probably as startled by me as I was by it, but the only thing worse than a giant spider under your pillow is knowing that giant spider is still somewhere in the room and you have no idea where.

That was it, limit reached, game over. I went outside, sought out the first person I could find, and begged for help.

Lessons learned from the grass hut on the Zambezi:

- A few of anything is much more manageable than an overabundance (think snowflake versus avalanche).
- I'm not nearly as okay with creepy-crawly things as I once thought.
- Pride is a dangerous thing.
- God has quite the sense of humor.

I had a painful lesson to learn and, because of my stubborn pride, I had to learn it the hard way. I share this with you hoping I can spare you your own nights with the bugs. I was proud of the thought that I was tough, that I could handle it out there—a little too proud. I was depending on my own strength and feeling really good about it. I suppose I liked it when people would ask how I do it; I could honestly tell them that it just didn't bother me. But

God knew that pride had to come down and He took care of it… handily. It was like He said, "Oh really? Try this!"

The problem with pride is it takes up all the space. I have an image in my mind of a spiky puffer fish. When I feel a little too pleased with myself, that fish is fully puffed. As self puffs up, there's no room for things like vulnerability, compassion, or humility. And there is certainly no room to notice the wonder around you when you are focusing on the wonder that is you. Pride demands nurturing, like a big baby. It can't afford to look bad or get caught with its pants down. And those spikes will eventually become a barrier between me and other people, me and joy, me and the good things God has planned.

There is no doubt this whole chilling experience was about God teaching me an important lesson because my coworkers in the other huts had no issues. Every hut was lovely and well maintained. This was about me. I sat under that mosquito net with my flashlight, reading my Bible and praying—hard. I had to forcefully shift my focus away from the nefarious plans of the insects surrounding me and onto something much larger and more important than myself. I got some sleep those nights, but not because of my own determination or mental strength; it was entirely with God's help.

Then, to top it all off, admitting my weakness and going out to ask the guys for help was like a sharp stick in the eye. I felt weak and embarrassed, and it was exactly what God knew I needed. I only felt a little better because they were as freaked out by it all as I was.

I learned a lot in that hut of bugs, but I still have a way to go. It isn't like I am completely finished with this battle against self. I am a strong person and I'm strong-willed; in many ways I'm grateful for both of these qualities. But our strengths can also be our weaknesses. I fight this battle every day, and I will do whatever it takes to win. The last thing I want is another night-with-the-bugs experience!

Your strength is a good thing; it's a gift from God, but strength must be balanced by an even stronger love and tempered with humility. When it's not, the result is pride, taking up all the space and limiting the joy in your life as well as keeping that joy from others. No one wants to spend much time with a prideful person. Love shrouded in pride is no love at all.

LOVE IS A BATTLEFIELD

In the immortal words of Pat Benatar, love is a battlefield. I love fiercely, and my goal, at least to the best of my feeble ability, is to love like Jesus does. That applies to me as a wife, a mother, a friend, and a leader. Loving others with God's love means love that is *strong* and *grounded by humility* because either without the other is incomplete.

I want to be strong, dependable, and firm in my convictions.

Ready and willing to tackle difficult challenges and to fight for those I love. All while remaining soft, approachable, flexible to the Holy Spirit's leading, and gentle in guidance and correction. I want the underlying strength to be wrapped in a lovely layer of kindness, keeping pride at bay.

When it comes to love, I also have to be prepared to lose a few battles. When that love isn't accepted or I end up with a few scrapes and bruises along the way, which is inevitable, it hurts. But I can't stop loving because of it. My adventures are worthless without love, and if I can help someone else experience the love of God that I have been blessed to walk in all of my life, it is worth the risk.

In order to love in this way, we need to make an important decision—we must choose to be unoffendable. I've been lovingly nudging you throughout our time together but I'm going to push harder on this one. This is worthy of a solid kick in the pants because this one change can lure out more wonder in your life than most. When we open our heart to love, there will be times when we get hurt. The question is, how does real love respond? Pride says, "I didn't deserve that" or "I need to get even." Love reminds us there are no perfect people, including ourselves, and we rarely know a person's true motives, so why not assume the best and keep our joy intact.

Laying down your pride and the right to be offended is much better than staying angry and always expecting the other shoe to drop. People make mistakes and loving people doesn't always go as planned, but as our daughter once said when she was little, "You can't wipe off the kiss, just the sloppy part. The love already soaked in." How great is that?

Life and love are messy and living in a state of constant offense is a surefire way to miss out on that joy you crave. Pride encourages us to get upset at all the wrong things. The right perspective helps us to realize we all face pain in our lives. Pride says I didn't deserve that while love says I'm no better than anyone else.

My very favorite adventures may surprise you because they aren't alligator hunts in the Amazon, camel rides at the pyramids, or hyenas scratching on my tent walls. In a world that is desperate for belonging and acceptance, my most memorable and rewarding experiences revolve around opportunities to love. These have filled my heart from corner to corner like nothing else and have ripped it from my chest, leaving me bleeding. Either way, nothing in my life has brought more wonder to life or been more fulfilling.

Hugging kids who have been brushed aside all their lives. Offering a loving touch to people in a leprosy village who have been declared "untouchables." Taking the time to listen to people who have never been heard. Seeing those who have felt invisible. Loving others so outweighs anything else that we could search for or desire. These are the adventures that set my mind where it should be—off myself and my desire to be lifted up, and back on the wonder of love.

STEP BY STEP

- Avoid your own "night with the bugs." Ask God to show you the areas of pride you need to deal with before He does it for you.
- Identify the specific people and situations where you want to love more like Jesus; tough and tender.
- Determine to be unoffendable today, then determine it again tomorrow and every day after that.
- Your next adventure: find someone in your world who needs to be seen or heard and go love them in that way.

CHAPTER 16

OUT OF THE NEST

The most difficult thing is the decision to act,
the rest is merely tenacity.
—Amelia Earhart—

It's time. You are ready to chase after wonder—and to make it a lifestyle, not just a onetime thing. You aren't simply visiting wonder; you are going to pursue it and live there. The time has come for you to step out toward all those amazing adventures ahead. Make them *your* adventures—not mine, not your parent's, or your friend's. So, let's wrap up our strategy and send you on your way. You may want to begin with a small step just to dip your toe into the water or your first step may be a bold leap. Either way, do something. You must do something.

Open the door to a new relationship, a new job, or a new

attitude. Do something wild or set aside some quiet time with God. Plan a trip—go around the world or around the block. Go out and help someone in need or stay in and pray like you mean it. Strike now while you are motivated and passionate. Otherwise, the crazy busy, hectic pace of life may squelch your adventures, squeeze out your joy, and roll right over your peace.

Too often our lifestyle simply isn't manageable. We're like hamsters on a wheel, running faster and faster but accomplishing little except for exhausting ourselves. It seems like we're doing more and more but enjoying life less and less. And there is certainly no time to sneak in a great adventure. What happens when that wheel continues to spin with you running and getting nowhere fast, month after month, year after year?

You've heard it before, but life is short. There will most likely come a time when I have to slow down. My goal is to maintain that adventure mentality as long as I possibly can, soaking up the wonder and experiencing more than enough joy for plenty to spill over. My specific adventures may need to adapt to new seasons of life, but I believe God has adventure and joy for us all whatever our circumstances may be. My intention is to take advantage of every moment I possibly can. For my life to get a little bit larger with each year that comes and passes. And it will be even more fun if you come along with me!

One of my very favorite promises of God is found in Jeremiah 29:13. It says, "You will seek me and find me, when you seek me with all your heart." The problem is we are often so busy *doing* what we think God wants that we neglect to *seek* Him. And that, my friends, is how years go by and nothing changes. That is how we get to the finish line and realize we haven't really lived at all, let alone basked in His wonder and accomplished everything we could have.

I love the New Year. It brings a freshness and new, exciting opportunities and challenges—at least that's how I like to look at it—and I don't want to miss a single one. With that in mind, many years ago I began using the New Year as a prompt to take a sort of inventory of my life, asking two important and challenging questions. Over the years this inventory has played an important role in many of my life decisions. It has served as a catalyst to move me when I felt complacent or too comfortable, and it has renewed my passion and determination when I needed to stay right where I was.

THE TWO-QUESTION INVENTORY

The first question is one I ask myself: "Why am I doing what I'm currently doing?" As we discussed earlier, motives matter. Even if I do what God wants me to but have the wrong motivation, it likely won't have the impact it should.

As a journalist, I love good follow-up questions, so here are some that help me to dial in my answer:

- Do I do this because I passionately believe in the purpose?
- Am I effective?
- Am I seeking glory for myself or for God?
- Am I serving others or am I acting selfishly?
- Do I need to tenaciously stay the course or am I resisting change because of insecurity?

If I am completely honest with myself, these answers tell me if I need to adjust my attitude or motives in order to seek God with an open heart.

The second question in my inventory is one I ask God: Am I doing what You want me to do? It's far too easy to continue doing what we have been, simply because it's what we know—it's comfortable. After all, if God asked us to do it before, it certainly must be what He wants now, right? Not necessarily. I may have been smack-dab in the center of God's will before, but seasons change, and God's purpose for that time or in that area may be fulfilled. He may be looking to do a new thing, to stretch me. Or He may want me to continue in the work He has given me without growing weary and with renewed commitment. The wonderful news is, either way, we're in an exciting place—either full of new vision or renewed passion.

A friendly warning—don't ask this question unless you're prepared for an answer. If you've already drawn the line at what you are willing to do or how far you will allow your adventures to take you, then it's best not to seek God's direction, because He will tell you, and disobedience is not fun. I've tried that route and learned His plan is much better, even though I may not realize it at the time.

Now may be the perfect time for your two-question inventory. You certainly don't need to wait for the New Year. It may be exactly the catalyst you need to jump-start your adventures. I understand it can be intimidating. You may wonder, "What will God ask me to do?" "What if I don't hear the answer?" Valid questions. But the bigger question is this: What will you miss if you don't ask?

CAUTION: CHANGE AHEAD

What if God does direct you toward a new adventure? What if you feel Him leading you to make a change? We're all different. If you're like me, you thrive on change. If you're like my husband, you flourish under the consistency of familiarity. The two of us together balance each other and make a good team. Where I may flit to something shiny and new, he holds my compass; and when he is hesitant to answer a new call, I'm there to pick up the phone. I have to avoid change for change's sake—seeking the rush of new adventure and moving before God tells me to. People who resist change must force themselves to step out of that comfort zone and go when God says go.

In our own way we all struggle with new beginnings; they take a great deal of faith. But without them, our progress is stunted. God never changes, but He does ask us to. Thankfully, He also walks with us every step of the way.

I remember a couple of times in particular when God was bringing change to my life, new adventures I didn't feel ready to face. The first came in my early twenties when I was working as a producer and reporter for a daily television talk show and was asked to become a cohost. I wanted to accept, but I was concerned I was too young. Was I ready? Would the audience accept me? I'm sorry to say I declined the opportunity. Not even two years later, the door opened again and this time I said yes. It was a wonderful experience that shaped the trajectory of my career, but who knows what I missed the first time around?

The second time was a year that brought a great deal of change to our family as we celebrated two graduations and a wedding. Our youngest daughter graduated high school and began college. Our oldest daughter graduated college, got married, and moved away. Perhaps the biggest challenge was one I did not at all expect—it was adjusting to the crazy woman who moved into our house. Somewhere in the midst of it all, an unpredictable woman on an emotional roller coaster came in and replaced the once steady cheerleader for progress and change. Yeah, it was me— *I* was the crazy lady.

She would be happy and then she would be weepy. She would trust God, then she would try to fix everything herself. And to top it all off, she referred to herself in the third person. So annoying.

As life and my role in it changed, I began to consider questions that surprised me. *Who am I now?* Our girls are now adults and don't need me in the same way: *Is my value based on being a mother?* I am getting older: *Is my worth based on youth or appearance?* I'm grateful for the wonderful opportunities God has given me: *But how long will I be able to gallivant around the globe? Is who I am based on what I do? Are my days of adventure nearing an end? Is my world of wonder about to grow smaller?*

This was all very unlike me, and I needed to evict that crazy woman. Like medicine for my soul, God gently reminded me as only He can that no change will ever alter who He says I am. He always has a good plan for me. He loves me, not because of what I do; my value is based on His unconditional love for me, and who I am, is His. I'm happy to report the steady cheerleader for progress returned and, for the most part at least, has held her ground. The adventures continue, and I do honestly believe they are getting even better!

With time I have grown to love the changes in my life, including my age. I appreciate all I've learned as well as the fact that now I have more experience and wisdom to offer. I've also learned it is okay not to have all the answers, to be vulnerable, and I'm much more comfortable with that than I have ever been. With each new stage comes new opportunities, lessons to learn, and adventures to relish. And I have much more ahead. Fortunately, the roller coaster of change never ends, and I wouldn't want it to. I just buckle in a little bit more tightly.

You are the perfect age for your adventure right now; you're not too young and not too old. Each phase of life brings something beautiful of its own, so much wonder to chase, if you are open to seeing it and open to change. Don't fight it; it's good stuff. Be grateful for who you are, what you've survived, and how far you've come. Trust God to use you as you are.

Years from now I don't want to look up and realize I missed great opportunities for even more wonder in my life and extra joy to splash out onto others. I don't ever want to say, "I wish I would have…" And because you have taken this journey with me, I know you're the kind of person who doesn't want that either.

A WORK OF ART

One last thing may be holding you back. You may be concerned you have nothing to offer. I keep a wonderful piece of geometric art in my office because it's beautiful and it inspires me. I brought it home from Rwanda and it's called *imigongo*, a traditional art form where women mix cow dung with ash and sculpt it into elaborate geometric patterns. They finish it in black and white or a touch of red. This art has been sold and displayed all over the world and can bring high ticket prices. Did you hear me? They take *cow poop* and make it beautiful and valuable. *Everyone* has something to offer.

Even if you feel a little bit like that cow poop, God sees a beautiful piece of art and wants to help you shape it into a masterpiece.

He knows your value, because He placed it inside of you first-hand. He looks at you and sees a work of wonder.

It's time for you to step out in faith. Come on friend, let's go chasing wonder together. Try something new. Look for the miracles around you; let those creative ideas flow; don't shy away from vulnerability; get a little uncomfortable at times and tell fear it won't stop you any longer. All you need to begin is at least one small step in the right direction and before you know it, you'll be chasing at a full run.

Open your heart to wonder and your life to big adventures. Fan that adventure mentality into full flame. Run from boredom and oblivion; no more days languishing in dissatisfaction on a road toward regret. I'm kicking you out of the nest—it's time to fly off to adventures of your own. Trust God for the extraordinary. Make your world big, chase down some wonder, seize that joy, and let the adventures begin!

ENCOURAGEMENT FOR YOUR ADVENTURES

You make known to me the path of life;
in your presence there is fullness of joy; at your
right hand are pleasures forevermore.
—Psalm 16:11—

There is no passion to be found playing small—
in settling for a life that is less than the one
you are capable of living.
—Nelson Mandela—

All life is an experiment.
The more experiments you make the better.
—Ralph Waldo Emerson—

"Who is like you, O LORD, among the gods?
Who is like you, majestic in holiness, awesome in
glorious deeds, doing wonders?"
—Exodus 15:11—

In the end, it's not the years in your life that count.

It's the life in your years.

—Abraham Lincoln—

What was wonderful about childhood is that anything

in it was a wonder. It was not merely a world full of

miracles; it was a miraculous world.

—G. K. Chesterton—

May the God of hope fill you with all joy

and peace in believing, so that by the power

of the Holy Spirit you may abound in hope.

—Romans 15:13—

You can't wait for inspiration;

you have to go after it with a club.

—Jack London—

ACKNOWLEDGMENTS

Writing this book was certainly an adventure and one I absolutely loved, because of the wonderful people who inspired me along the way and helped me make it to the finish line.

This book could not have happened without my amazing family—each one of you! I am so very grateful for my husband, Tim, who is the gallant sidekick beside me through most of my adventures. I love you so very much!

To our beautiful daughters, Taylor and Morgan, you have absolutely been my greatest adventure and brought more wonder into my life than I ever dreamed possible. Morgan, thank you for challenging me to write my book while you wrote your dissertation. We did it! I am so very proud of you both and love you to pieces!

I am deeply grateful to several people who lit a fire underneath me. My dear friends Erin Cluley, Jai Williams, and Megan Rossman, thank you for believing I had a message to share and for pushing me until I did. Love you all. And Chad Daniel, your tender words, "Get off your butt and write!" inspired me to put those first elusive words on the page.

My heartfelt appreciation to my boss and friend Joyce Meyer. Thank you for trusting me with so much and for being the catalyst that brought so many of my adventures to life these last eighteen years. Your kind words written in the foreword brought me to tears. And to Dan Meyer, who has been one of my strongest advocates, relentlessly believing in me and never failing to make me laugh. My love and sincerest gratitude to both of you.

Susan Crumley, Terry Redman, and Paul Huse, I thank you for lending your expertise and your encouragement. I am beyond grateful for your enthusiasm for this project. And Amanda Bjornson, you make every day look so much better!

My heartfelt gratitude goes to the team at Worthy Publishing/ Hachette Book Group. Daisy Blackwell Hutton, Jeana Ledbetter, and Morgan Rickey, you are some of the kindest, most sincerely encouraging people I ever could have asked to work with. Thank you for believing in the possibilities and helping to mine the best out of these words. And to my literary agent, Tom Winters, thank you for your patience through my barrage of questions and for making this dream a reality.

Finally, thank You, God, for overwhelming me with Your goodness and wonder!

NOTES

CHAPTER 1
1 https://www.merriam-webster.com/dictionary/wonder

CHAPTER 9
1 http://gss.norc.org/getthedata/Pages/Home.aspx
2 https://worldhappiness.report/ed/2019/the-sad-state-of-happiness-in-the
-united-states-and-the-role-of-digital-media/

CHAPTER 10
1 https://www.lexico.com/en/definition/miracle

ABOUT THE AUTHOR

GINGER STACHE is an Emmy Award–winning documentarian, writer, and television producer who is just as comfortable in the African bush as she is on a TV set. She has traveled the world sharing stories of amazing people who overcome incredible odds. Ginger loves to uncover the best in people, the creative approach, beauty in all things, and joy in each day.

She is the chief creative officer of Joyce Meyer Ministries and can be seen on Joyce Meyer's *Enjoying Everyday Life* program and heard hosting Joyce Meyer's *Talk It Out* podcast. She is also a mom, an unashamed sci-fi nerd, an adventurer, and a leader who believes in the power of compassion, inspiring people, and sharing Jesus by telling great stories. She lives in Missouri with her husband and one small, twitchy puppy. They have two beautiful grown daughters and two spectacular grandchildren.

Keep up with Ginger's adventures by following her on Instagram and Facebook @gingerlstache and her website: gingerlstache.com.